D1796034

© 2019 Mickeal Milocco Borlini, Lelio di Loreto. Tutti i diritti riservati.

ISBN 978-0-244-15429-5
Lulu.com

The authors have signed a release in which they take full responsibility for their text and the images included in their section.

For any information or mistake please contact first urbancorporis@gmail.com or info@iuvas.org

Cover and last pages image:
Eric Fischer, Is this the structure of New York City? Broadway as the spine is not difficult to believe. Data from the Twitter streaming API (10000 points, 30000 vectors). Base map from OpenStreetMap, CC-BY-SA. https://www.flickr.com/photos/walkingsf/6747484741 1/2019

URBAN CORPORIS • THE CITY WITHIN

A book of Architecture, Art, Philosophy and Urban studies to nourish the Urban Body.

By Mickeal Milocco Borlini, Lelio di Loreto

EDITORIAL BOARD

Mickeal Milocco, Ph.D., Architecture
Lelio di Loreto, Ph.D., Architecture

SCIENTIFIC BOARD

Chiara Giorgetti, Professor, Fine Arts, Brera's Academy of Fine Arts, Milan
Nicola Vazzoler, Ph.D. Urban Studies, Post-Doc Researcher, RomaTre, Rome
Fabrizio Zanni, Professor, Architecture and Urban Planning, Politecnico di Milano
Lorenzo Giacomini, Professor, Aesthetics, Politecnico di Milano
Fabrizia Berlingieri, Post- Doc Researcher, Adj. Professor of Architecture and Urban Planning, Politecnico di Milano
Lorenzo Bagnoli, Ph.D., Architecture, President at I.U.V.A.S.

A book by

www.iuvas.org

Partner

www.generazioneurbana.it

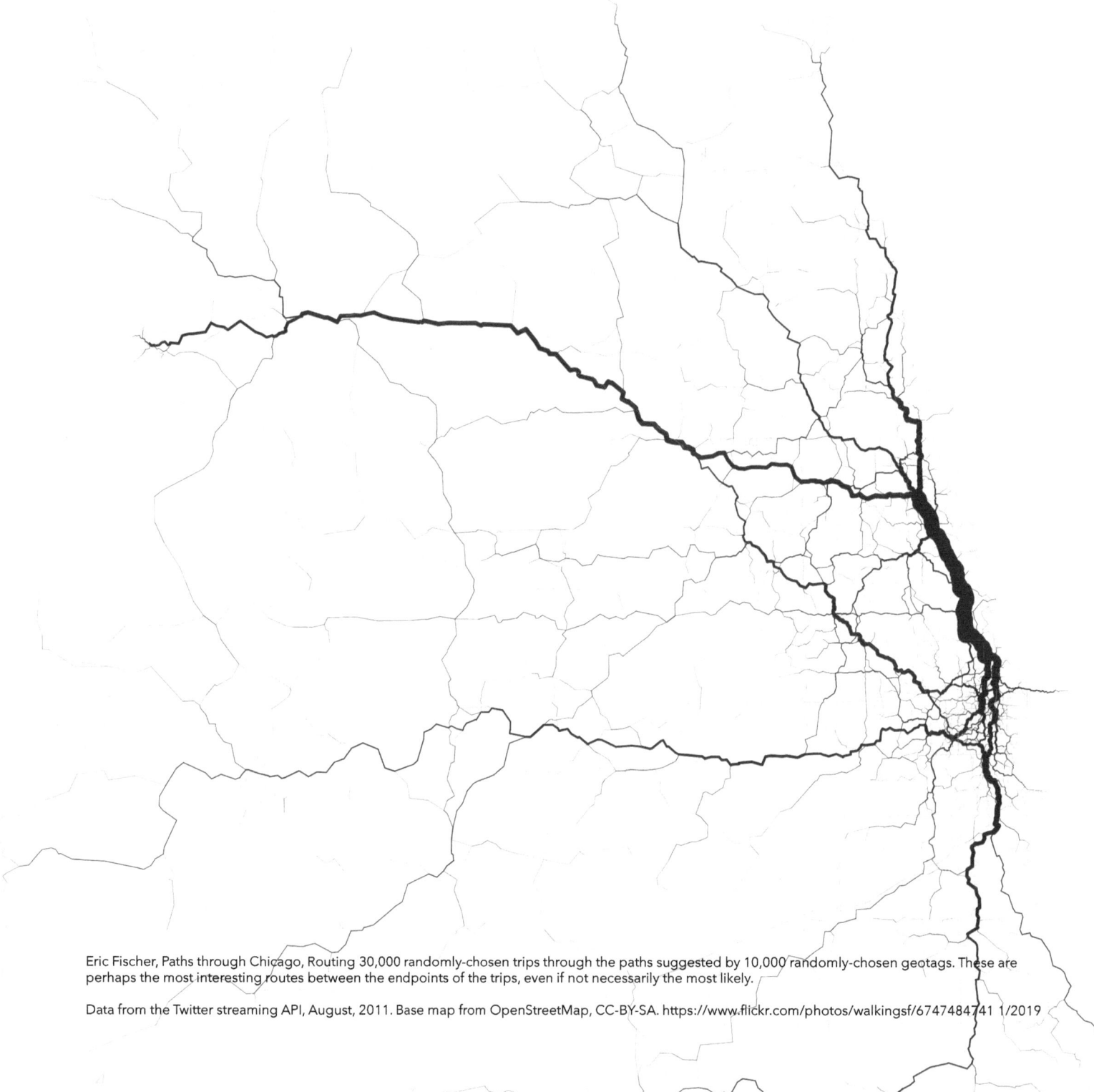

Eric Fischer, Paths through Chicago, Routing 30,000 randomly-chosen trips through the paths suggested by 10,000 randomly-chosen geotags. These are perhaps the most interesting routes between the endpoints of the trips, even if not necessarily the most likely.

Data from the Twitter streaming API, August, 2011. Base map from OpenStreetMap, CC-BY-SA. https://www.flickr.com/photos/walkingsf/6747484741 1/2019

A BOOK OF ARCHITECTURE, ART, PHILOSOPHY AND URBAN STUDIES TO NOURISH THE URBAN BODY

INDEX

INDEX

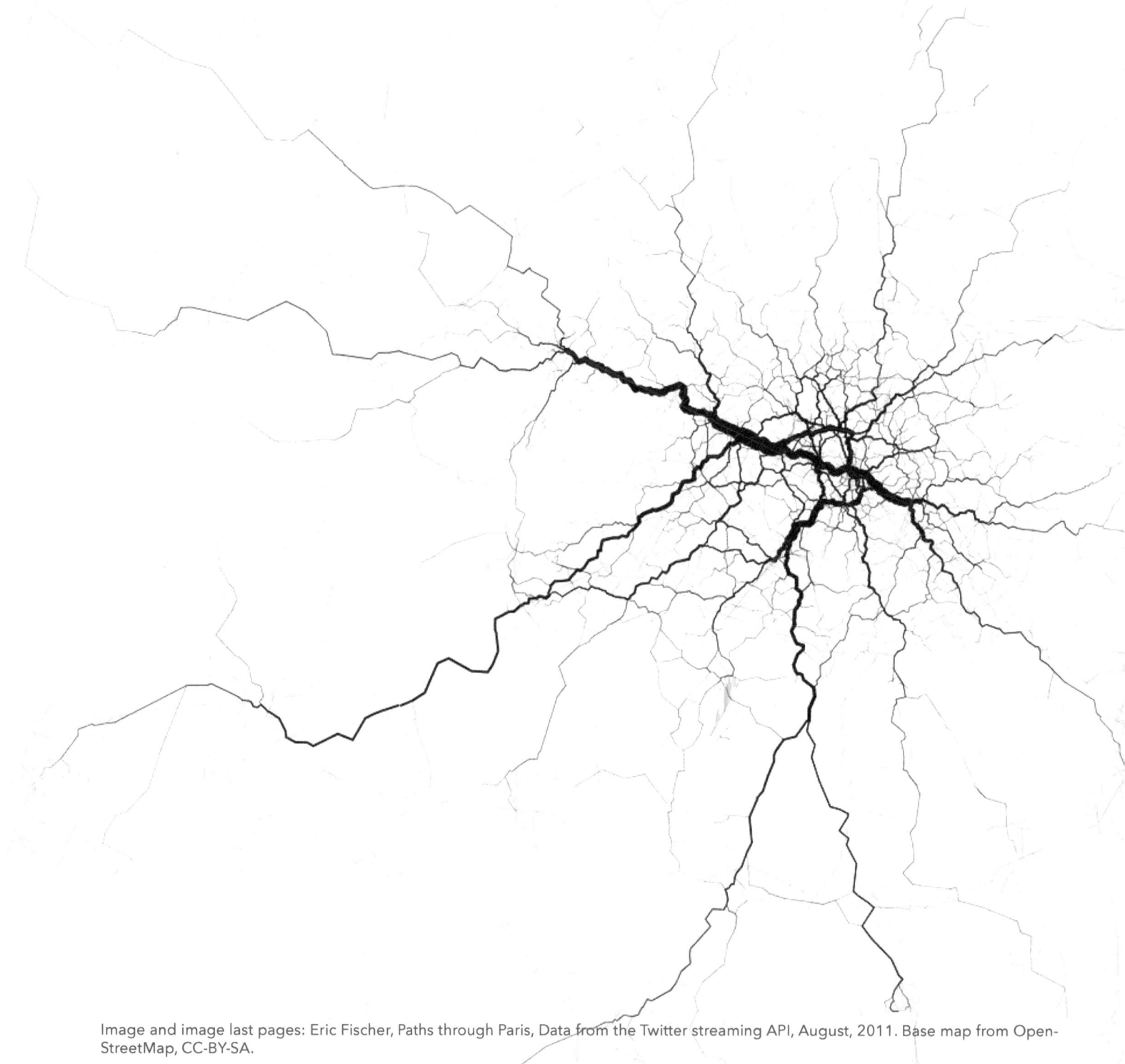

Image and image last pages: Eric Fischer, Paths through Paris, Data from the Twitter streaming API, August, 2011. Base map from Open-StreetMap, CC-BY-SA.

INCIPIT

This *pamphlet* brings together the contributions of architects, researchers and artists from all over the world. The common ground of discussion is the city analyzed in its less explored "folds" becoming the ground for experimentation and research.
The work is divided into three parts:
Theories - Report - Visions.

The three categories bring together authors who have had, in their specificity, a reading experience of the city belonging to a similar field of action.

The Theories part has a theoretical approach overlapping with an operative study of possible interventions in the urban fabric; an historical analysis seems to play a key role in all theses.

The Report focuses on the residual spaces of the city; the relationship between art and architecture seems to be the solution of this spatial rebus, even if it leads to always different results.

Visions is a collection of future projections, fast images and critical readings of the city. Through drawings, photomontages and photographs we tried to expose the most significant aspects of different urban situations.

These materials together do not want to give solutions but they want to ask new questions, being conscious that curisioty remains necessary for any kind of progress.

THEORIES

The subsoil in history or the history in the subsoil?

Lelio di Loreto, Ph.D.

Author Bio

lelio di loreto was born in rome in 1989. He graduated from Sapienza, faculty of architecture "Valle Giulia" with five-year master degree in 2014. recently he has developed special interest for design and construction processes and he founded the line_a design group. He is a Ph.D in Architecture since 2018.

Starting from the dual nature of the soil, defined in an upper part "soil" and in a lower "subsoil, my interpretation suggests two formae urbis that in this writing will take the name respectively of "forma urbis" and "sub forma urbis", in other words, two real city plans that run parallel to each other and that meet through folds and connections in rare and exceptional points. However, even if these points are studied, designed and known in all their vertical and horizontal dimensions, the rest of the "sub forma urbis" is quite understudied, poorly designed and, in many cases, unknown even if it does exist and it has valuable artistic and historical content.

This lower part of the city has the same problems as the first: planning, the correlation between pre-existence-new, services, connections, relations.

If the forma urbis is subjected to hyper-analytic processes, while it needs some healthy spontaneous entropy (which is not illegal), the sub forma urbis is instead hypo-analyzed by fragments and, as mentioned, in some cases it is totally ignored as if it did not exist until the moment of the excavation.
As emerged during the seminar, it is very rare to have sections of the city with a detailed study of the subsoil but in my opinion it is even more grave that there are no floor plans that accurately document everything that takes place in the lower ground floor in order to to be able to design the latter and not to have unpleasant surprises in the design of the upper floor.
Taking as an example the Italian situation that has to do with the most complex and delicate soil in Europe for physical characteristics and for the almost omnipresent possibility of finding objects of artistic historical value, it is natural to wonder if it is right to dig unconsciously and then be forced to destroy or cement (as it often happens) or worse, to bury or make unexpected design changes, rather than digging and designing with the awareness of what already exists in the subsoil. Why cannot we plan, and therefore know, the sub forma urbis in order to exalt its values, as they are functional or artistic historical? As can be derived from the above, it is possible to combine the types of sub forma urbis into two macro-groups. The first macro group includes cities with high-quality subsoil or functional potential.

The second one includes cities which have a subsoil characterized by a very relevant archaeological presence and therefore with a cultural vocation. Specifically, I have been interested in a city belonging to the second macro group in order to explore the possibilities that can be derived from the prudent use of a pre-existing resource. The element of major interest is the possibility of expanding the city without the need to build or demolish, to occupy the land, to create new infrastructures with a strong environmental impact and the list goes on. On the contrary, with the intervention I propose, we will only have to find out, reuse and relate the above and below without creating or destroying.

Recent history gives examples of enlightened interventions of this kind to us. The first example that I propose is Palestrina, which was on fire and destroyed in 1437; fifty years later it was reconstructed topographically and intellectually, regenerating itself and then its architectures starting from the ground conformation and from what remained beneath it. " Palestrina has regenerated after each destruction. The architecture of the ground, in this case, surpasses the architecture of the buildings, and this is the true sign of intellectual growth: while the architectural styles change, the nature of the soil remains."(F. Venezia) In Palestrina the crankcase, the ramps, the connections and the substructures are kept; the extreme synthesis between archetypal symbols and technique. This happens to many medieval cities and it is something that has continued over time. After the destruction of the Second World War, it is precisely the soil that is made visible and returns to being a protagonist, but the institutions have blocked the regenerative force of the city. Palestrina has rege-

And, lo ! toward us in a bark
Comes on an old man, hoary white with eld,
Crying, " Woe to you, wicked spirits ! "

Canto III., lines 76-78.

nerated after each destruction. Not after this one. This example follows variations on the theme of which the unusual classicism - romantic of Piranesi and the rational genius of Le Corbusier emerge. The first proposes visions that make their strength disproportionally realistic; the underground Piranesi vision of the "Imaginary Prisons" is evidently something that is much closer to the concept of the sublime than to the concept of architecture. However, he is the first to think and design such complex connection networks in an underground world. The second one gives us yet another lesson of architecture in the design for the Swiss Pavilion of the University of Paris, the building starts at a simple and quick construction up to the unforeseen discovery of old quarries dating back to the construction of ancient neighbourhoods of Paris. However, the architect is ready in his poetic reaction. The cross-section of the project is determined by the presence of the cavity. This image looks as visionary as the Piranesian prisons. It envisions a future in which Le Corbusier pilotis converse with the pre-existence in mutual respect.

It is on this concession of interchange that the project of Bernard Tschumi for the Acropolis Museum of Athens is based on and the projects of Francesco Venezia for a house in Palazzolo Acreide and the restoration of the ancient centre of Salerno.

Tschumi's project is interesting for the positioning of the pillars inside the ruins present in the subsoil but the real innovation is the relationship that creates with the underlying floor that becomes, at least visually, an integral part of the museum. The sensitivity of Venice towards the subject treated is already evident in the writing for the subsoil of Naples. It is interesting to note the role that is attributed to the ground of the two projects: in the first one the pre-existence becomes the access from a square to a lower level compared to the building; in the second one, instead, a large building is created, almost an out of scale compared to the inhabited centre, but its role is to gather all the functions, it is a "world building" that in its form is coherently connected to the ground making it accessible in all its different heights. If in Palestrina the city evolves according to the very efficient connection system, here an efficient connection system is created in an existing city.

It should not seem strange to think of a design of the underground, it refers to a very remote condition of building and living. The return to an interest in the subsoil is an authentic expression of modernity. The architecture of the soil gives an artificial order to nature and having a character of particular persistence is not related to the time but to the nature of the site. The reconsideration of the architecture of the soil can have a decisive influence on a new urban theory. Urban planning practice will be forced to give the right value to the ground because it will become a rare resource.

IMAGES

1. James St. John Segui
Canyon passage (Boone Avenue, Mammoth Cave, Kentucky, USA) 21, Attribution 2.0 Generic (CC BY 2.0)

2. Gustave Doré's illustration to Dante's Inferno. Plate IX: Canto III: Arrival of Charon. "And lo! towards us coming in a boat / An old man, hoary with the hair of eld, / Crying: 'Woe unto you, ye souls depraved!'" (Longfellow's translation) "And, lo! toward us in a bark / Comes an old man, hoary white with eld, / Crying "Woe to you, wicked spirits!" (Cary's translation), 1857, Public domain, {{PD-US}} https://commons.wikimedia.org/wiki/File:Gustave_Doré_-_Dante_Alighieri_-_Inferno_-_Plate_9_(Canto_III_-_Charon).jpg

Among the perimeters
Possible renegotiations of soil and subsoil space: the open block

Mickeal Milocco Borlini, Ph.D.

Author Bio

mickeal milocco was born in palmanova (ud), in 1985.
He pursues his artistic and technical interests attending the art institute "giovanni sello" in udine. He graduated in architecture at Politecnico di Milano University and he has a Ph.D in architecture (Sapienza, Rome).

The goal of this text is to analyze the usefulness of the open-block through some significant examples. Starting from the ideas of "open block" by C. de Portzamparc, it is possible to understand the need to create new collective and public places between the existing urban fabric in order to improve the possibilities of social aggregation. Trough redefining the perimeters of the urban volumes and trough hybrid spaces that break through the cordons of the perimetric architecture, we would proceed towards the development of in-between spaces, which restore continuity with the city. In order to create new social places in the existing local fabric we should focus on the urban redevelopment that redefines the perimeters of the buildings. That it is possible by "reopening the courts" and by developing fluid and continuous areas that prolong the urban fabric and reconnect it to a ground/underground circulation system, without interruptions.

Open the block. Do we renegotiate space?

To fully understand the meaning of "open block" we must introduce its opposite concept.

What is the block?

block
noun UK /blɒk/ US /blɑːk/

mainly US - the distance along a street from where one road crosses it to the place where the next road crosses it, or one part of a street like this, especially in a town or city; a square group of buildings or houses with roads on each side; a large, usually tall building divided into separate parts for use as offices or homes by several different organizations or people;

verb [T] UK /blɒk/ US /blɑːk/

to prevent movement through something; to be between someone and the thing they are looking at, so that they cannot see; to stop something from happening or succeeding;

(Cambridge Business English Dictionary © Cambridge University Press)

From the above mentioned definition we understand how the block not only delimits a perimeter making it almost inaccessible, but also shrinks some social and passing interactions. As Roccella G. recognizes, this also derives from the fact that «*the ground floors of the buildings are occupied by public [and commercial] functions [...] and on the top the residencial stories. [This is based] on a vertical zooning that produces cities with closed levels, which tend not to communicate with each other. The public and the private sector, therefore, remain well divided, regulated by the properties, in which the inward public spaces remain for their exclusive use»*(2011). From the words of the same author we deduce that we need to design new inclusive and non-exclusive spaces of relationship that allow the interfacing of several urban areas starting from the street level. The "intermediate" spaces, the terrains vagues and the areas in great deterioration of the metropolis need to be reconnected to the urban system of public spaces, decreeing new unexpected spatial devices, new meeting places and neighborhood activities. The purpose of this text is to underline the importance of enhancing accessibility while discouraging the urban enclaves. It is possible to intervene on the urban fabric through the hybridization of vertical and horizontal systems, reconnecting the gaps of urban routes in order to renegotiate the space from an administrative and social point of view (Roccella, 2011).

Talking about the îlot ouvert (Accorsi, 2010), it is mandatory to mention the person who theorized it and put it into practice: Christian de Portzamparc. The open block is an architectural and urban instrument that solves many problems related to the caesura decreed by urban enclaves. As the architect himself acknowledges in an inter-

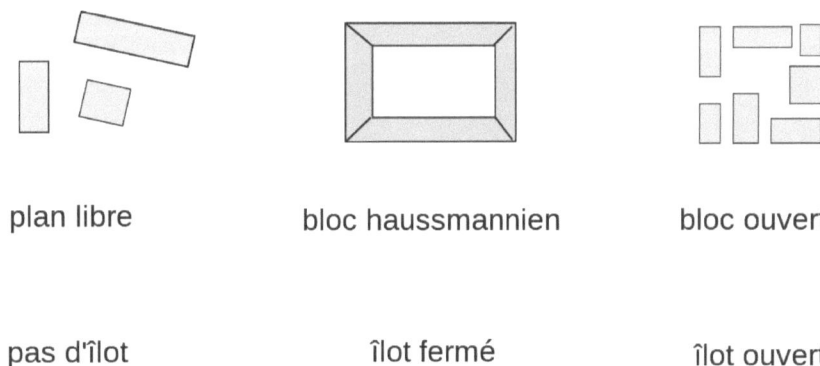

plan libre   bloc haussmannien   bloc ouvert

pas d'îlot   îlot fermé   îlot ouvert

view on the "Giornale dell'Architettura," the open-block undoubtedly allows the permeability through neighborhoods and it improves social interactions thanks to the opening of interior spaces towards the outside world, without creating caesuras that were previously established by continuous facades (Desmoulins, 2010). The architect began his experiments in the seventies with the projects for the Hautes-Formes and than successfully continued until the general planning of the Massena district in Paris through new construction rules and through the implementation of plans that fully reflected the idea of the open block - the "open district" in this case - thus generating a new urban typology (Accorsi, 2010). Porosity and openness towards the city are undoubtedly the key words of Portzamparc's projects. In the contemporary city it is now impossible to intervene on an urban scale without taking into account the differences between

the urban and social fabric. In view of the above considerations it is clear that architectural experimentation should focus on a greater use of open systems especially where there is a need for architectural regeneration or reconversion. Taking into account the social aspects, the new planning should make the urban areas (such as the block) once again permeable, going towards what Portzamparc himself calls mixitè, that can be social or functional. This strategy would allow a new translation of the aggregative spaces that reopen themselves from closed sites towards a more fluid, dynamic and interconnected city system. In support of this thesis we can summarize the considerations of I. Santarelli (2014) in the article "Abitare a corte. Reinterpretazioni contemporanee del blocco residenziale del blocco" where, in addition to Portzamparc ideas, she cites other designers who have experimented with different scales the subjects of this paper.

The author recalls the projects of Renzo Piano (Central Saint Giles of London) and Carlos Ferrater (Villa Olimpica, Barcellona) in which both designers break through the perimeters of the block through "architectural gestures", inserting passages of different depth, allowing an increased porosity and permeability. Those projects give back to the community a space that used to be private, closed breaking through a formal rule in the volumetric system, allowing a regained horizontal permeability (Santarelli, 2014). Apparently, it is not enough to think of the mixture between public and private in a horizontal sense only but also vertically. The thickness of the ground needs to

be considered in order to make the system more complex and at the same time more fluid, thus creating continuity between exterior and interior, above and below, in every single direction.

Soil and open block

Assuming that the concept of the open-block is fully acquired, it is possible to say that the use of the ground can be introduced in this discourse. The soils becomes a necessity to solve permeability issues especially when there is a need to operate on existing blocks. Thanks to the use of the first layer of soil it is possible to open the quads by digging and reconnecting internal courts with the exterior space. Hence it is possible to create new areas of aggregation and commer-

cial business in the subsoil itself. It is also possible to bring light to the underground services (trough gaps in the ground), in order to process them as general public space with trees, paths and benches. It is thus possible to reconnect areas that no longer need to be hidden within rigid courts, which can be renegotiated with the city. To make this possible we need to stop thinking two-dimensionally only, and starting to elaborate space in a three-dimensional way. The Open block should use the "Y" coordinate both above and below the ground line. This would create the connection areas at many heights (layers) that would allow a better use of space, especially on existing "blocks". In this way it is feasible to think of a continuous union of blocks (even between the ground) towards a

system represented by dynamic, fluid, porous, and continuous places as discussed at the beginning of this paper. An example is the Shanghai Greenland Center of Nikken Sekkei. The project occupies a very large quad and holds three tower buildings (offices and houses) that fit on a green slab which multiplies the walkable levels and consequentially their use. Crossings are guaranteed by cuts on the slab and uncovered routes as well as by the volumes below the plate; those ones merge commercial services and a direct connection to the metropolitan service. In summary, the area becomes a *«green urban valley a street landscape park»* (Sekkei, 2018), where the open block manifests itself on all spatial coordinates.

Conclusion

The most interesting outcome of the open block seem to reside in the continuous confrontation with the city through the thresholds of passage from a universe to the other: public, semi-public and private spaces. There emerges the strong ability to continuously re-configure the compositional principle in an attempt to respond to social issues, integration and livability in order to move towards an integrated city aimed at improving the problems of the diffused city. This urban vision has a fluid and porous system that continually re-negotiates its space with its citizens becoming a possible outcome in the near hereafter; the open block remains the fundamental principle to be declined while searching for new "compositional devices" for the "fluid" cities of the future.

BIBLIOGRAPHY

Bugatti A., Progettare il sottosuolo - nella città densa e nel paesaggio, Maggioli Editore, Milano, 2010

De Cesaris A., Il progetto del suolo-sottosuolo, Gangemi, Roma, 2012

Florio R., Christian de Portzamparc. Disegno e forma dell'architettura per la città, Officina, 1997

Roccella G., Abitare la città multilivello. Verso spazi pubblici più integrati, sostenibili, vivibili, Assegnista di Ricerca Post-Doc in Composizione Architettonica e Urbana, Dipartimento di Progettazione Architettonica e Disegno Industriale, Politecnico di Torino.

Valli M., Quaranta domande a Christian de Portzamparc, Clean, 1999

Zanni F., Infra-luoghi, Maggioli Editore, collana Politecnica, 2010

Zanni F. (a cura di), URBAN HYBRIDIZATION, Maggioli, Milano 2012

Accorsi F., L îlot ouvert de Christian de Portzamparc, Semapa, Paris 2010

Desmoulins C., Portzamparc: il mio isolato aperto è sempre la ricetta migliore per una città viva, Il giornale dell'architettura, 2010 Interviste, 821

Santarelli I., Abitare A Corte. Riletture Contemporanee Dell'isolato Residenziale A Blocco, Focus Architettura,focusarchitettura.wordpress.com, 2014

Nikken Sekkei "Shanghai Greenland Center " 14 Nov 2018. ArchDaily. Accessed 16 Dec 2018. <https://www.archdaily.com/905876/shanghai-greenland-center-nikken-sekkei/> ISSN 0719-8884

IMAGES

1. The three types of urban blocks ("îlots") according to Christian de Portzamparc. Drawing by User:Thbz, march 2006. Category:Christian de Portzamparc (CC BY-SA 3.0) https://fr.wikipedia.org/wiki/Fichier:Trois-blocs.svg

2. Central St. Giles Court, designed by Renzo Piano. Camden Town, London, UK, 31 July 2011, 08:59:49, Source - Flickr: Central St. Giles Court, Author: Peter Alfred Hess, Creative Commons Attribution 2.0 Generic license, from http://flickr.com/photo/22799676@N03/6024876083

3. Interior courtyard of Central Saint Giles in London, 28 January 2011, 17:04:22, Source - Flickr: Central Saint Giles, Author: Garry Knight, Creative Commons Attribution-Share Alike 2.0 Generic license, from http://flickr.com/photo/8176740@N05/5407174769

Marcel Duchamp is our guide
A new urban ecology in Spanish contemporary architecture

Giulio Bassanello

Author Bio

Giulio Bassanello is a 26 years old Milanese architect. He studied at the Universidade Lusíada de Lisboa and at Politecnico di Milano, where he graduated in 2017 and licensed in 2018. Through the years, some of his career projects have been published and exhibited, and his Master thesis about the historical centre of Caltagirone, Sicily, was the starting point for the proposal of a strategic urban regeneration plan in current development together with Studio di Architettura Carlo Alberto Maggiore, where he trained during and after his studies. Since 2018 he lives in Olot, Spains, where he works at RCR Arquitectes.

«Marcel Duchamp is our guide»[1]

Intervention in the urban context needs a proper consciousness, rife with ecological sense, which has nothing to do with the 'junglism' that is taking over some branches of contemporary architecture, pushed by self-celebration or a mediatic mindset instead of true interest for the building's role in the city, meant as the coexistence between citizens and buildings. If, in fact, while attempting to integrate nature and architecture is fair and comprehensible, we can't deny observing a certain tendency to conceal architecture, if not a negation of architecture itself through nature (Biraghi 2017); it is a misconception, or, in the worst perspective, a trick that publicly proclaims and aims to care for the city, and instead hides poorly made up concrete. The care for the city that we propose has its only interest in the quality and use of urban space, and saves the meaning of the word "ecology" meant as the study of interactions among organisms and their environment: for an effective urban environment schematization, the archetype is the *Nuova Topografia di Roma* (1748), through which Giambattista Nolli undressed the city, drawing its hybrid spaces in between the black urban tissue and the white unbuilt (as *Piazze*, *Strade* e *Vicoli*): they are the ground floors of religious and civic buildings such as *Cappelle*, *Chiese de Secolari o con Monasteri Conventi Ospizi & C*, *Collegi e Seminari*, *Luoghi Pubblici*, *Oratorj*, *Ospizi Regolari senza Chiesa*, *Ospizi Secolari*, *Palazzi*, *Spedali* e *Torri*. Such a monumental survey of the articulation of black and white boundary, even if restricted to the two-dimensional plan, tells us much about the dialogue between shapes, while at the same time unveils their use.

Interest for the interaction between buildings and people, therefore, is interest for what happens when the border dividing black and white moves, distorts, blurs, and when the parts mutually pour, invade, fracture: as for the sculpture and lithography of Basque artist Eduardo Chillida, among an "enigmatic limit" between full space and void space, "two things touch each other but remain different, transform one another" (Chillida 2010, p. 86). Architecture that shows the greatest attention to the ecological issue in the last few decades is the outcome of the experimentation that thrived in the Iberian area, where an already strong sensitivity for the dimensional scarcity reveals itself, together with a conscious inclination towards a smart use of space. Historian and critic Fernando Espuelas, in a lecture about Ragusa, defined the city as an *objet trouvé*, giving a Duchampian and ecological vision, investing the city in the act of transformation itself and, moreover, explaining how the city can be transformable not by substitution but by resemanticization, refunctionalization, rehabilitation. Following such a principle, architecture can at the same time make its own space and make space for others, amplifying the city's public significance and collective dimension, not by camouflage, but by becoming city.

With the *Planos Especiales de Reforma Interior* ("PERI BA189-2", 1997) for the Ciutat Vella, EMBT Studio guided, in an ecological way, the recent town planning of Barcelona: the operation was developed by Enric Miralles and Benedetta Tagliabue as an alternative to the previous plans ("PERI BA189", 1986), that prescribed for wide spaces and straight lines to breach the city's tissue in several areas. The two architects, with the purpose of reproducing the old town's pattern, conceived a small scale intervention characterized by "construction continuity, interrupted perspectives and the street as unique fundamental space" (Muxi 2005, p. 65). The comparison between the two solutions, despite a few years' difference, shows the reach of the Miralles-Tagliabue project, an urban plan focused on points, dictating the pre-existences' rehabilitation, a hybridation with the new in a sort of collage-operation, and the connection between public and private spaces thanks to a system of dilatation shaping the urban tissue. The will to reconstruct the old morphology shows up in the further proposals for the architectural scale by Bravo & Contepomi, Fuses y Viader, and Aranyó, Ensenyat y Tarrida. The historical towns' complexity is achieved through differences in the plan, in the height and in the treatment of the façades, which, in turn, interact with the surviving skin of the demolished buildings. This gaze penetrates the neighborhood

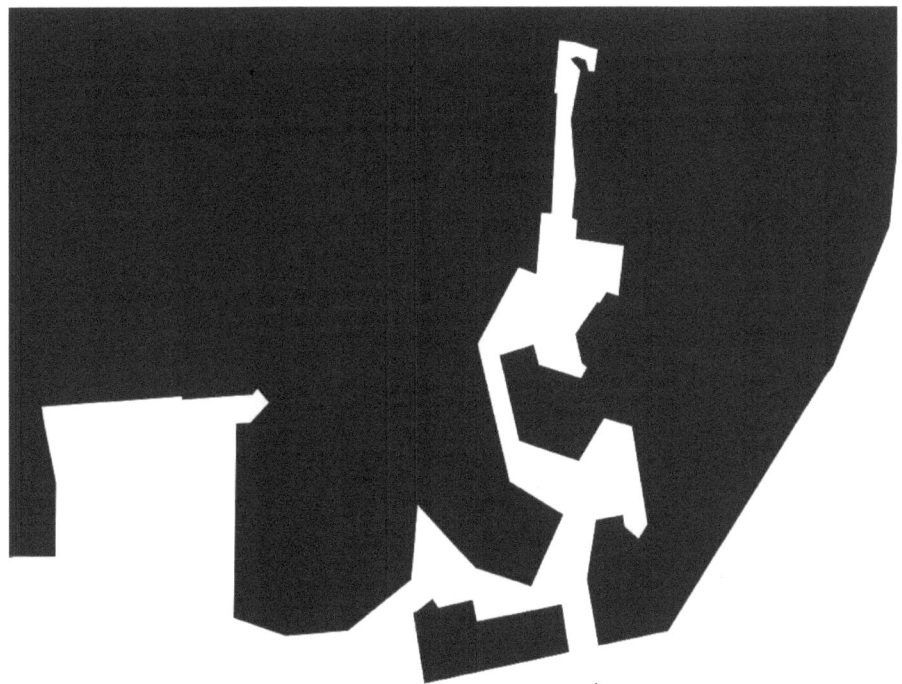

through irregularities and hybrids. The pre-existences and the self-imposed restrictions of the Miralles-Tagliabue *Planos* are elevated to become resources, but what makes it a successful project is the attention given to intermediate spaces: staircases, accesses, passages and underpasses, the new constructions 'granularity', the quality of the new street enlargements.

In a similar way, Josep Llinas succeeds in instilling in the exterior and public face of his projects an extraordinary plasticity, thanks to the public space design – we could call it 'air design' – that results in a meticulous shaping of the *manzana* (the block): the erosion of built mass is the direct aftermath of the urban project. As a mason, Llinas

doesn't only articulate the Chillidian limit, "real protagonist of the space" (Chillida 2010, p. 35), at the ground floor, but also gives a volumetric answer to the surrounding space depending on the context: besides his Barcelona projects, the cultural municipal complex "L'Atlàntida" in Vic (2010) is a model soil occupation, creating a relationship between the established tissue and a transformation area through the connection of different altitudes, and through the design of a public open 'pocket', sometimes covered, with respect to street access and the southern natural merge towards the river. Once again, from the planimetric irregular system of the voids, an ecological awareness emerges

and aspires to extend the open and public space right inside the borders of the built space.

Many projects by Rafael Moneo explain the importance of reading the city in an ecological sense as a guide for design. Examples include the turned façade of the Murcia Town Hall (1998), which doesn't align to any existing building, but has adapted instead to the square imagined by the architect; shreds of Cartagena gaining a new meaning around the renewed archaeological area (2008); the Congress Hall in Toledo (2009) meandering, and not hiding, in the topography and among the walls, integrating in the landscape and in the city struc-

ture. Moneo has always highlighted a tension between the answers given by the site and the importance of the architect's invention, so that he can take care of the city with buildings that don't impose shapes but adapt to urban attributes, realizing new sceneries; this was since accomplished with the Edificio Bankinter in Madrid (1976), doubled and opened in order to relate on two sides with residential buildings and a XIX century palace and with the Ayuntamiento of Logroño (1980), that generated a rotated square in relation to the urban grid, or with L'Illa Diagonal in Barcelona (1993) that, besides its scale, becomes city by breaking up the vol-

ume both in height and depth. In all these projects, the ground floor is made permeable through cuts and folds. Other architects' work on interstitial spaces, such as Nieto Sobejano with the San Telmo Museum in San Sebastian (2001) that, embedded between the former convent and the hill, makes its own space favoring horizontality and finds harmony with the duplicity of the place, or as José María Sánchez García in the intervention for the Diana Roman Temple rehabilitation in Merida (2011), eroding the mediocre surroundings in order to let the monument breathe, freeing the ground floor and alternating solid and void public spaces at the temple's basement height.

Those who better represent this ability to intervene in urban contexts, rethinking the ideas of "outside" and "inside", are RCR Arquitectes Aranda Pigem and Vilalta, whose sensitivity leads to extraordinary results with regards to built space quality. Their architecture is deeply tied to the territory and dissolves ingeniously the dividing line between interior and exterior, public and private, open and closed. The Sant Antoni – Joan Oliver Library in Barcelona (2007) was thought out as a portal through the built front, leading to the heart of the *manzana*: both in section and in plan, the architectural action is comparable to a breach, as an excavation becoming an extension of public space. Similarly, La Lira Theatre intervention in Ripoll (2005), connecting the sides of Ter river, builds a pass-through void, an entrance to the city centre, an introvert architecture with inner façades. The plan is eloquent and meaningful: a laceration in the urban pattern. The abandoned area, formerly occupied by La Lira Theatre, was found meaningless and returned to the citizens, making a theatre out of the city and a public space out of the building.

Architecture must take care of the city and its inhabitants, and cannot hide behind ideologies and artificial vests or claim absolute autonomy, celebrating a personality or a tendency. Spanish sensitivity teaches us how architecture can link its interiors with the city, or how architecture can become city; it ultimately tells us how to improve human daily life. Chillida, during his life, often questioned if there is something like a limit for the spirit. Espuelas implicitly and partially answered, defining void as "knowledge matter" (Espuelas 2001, p. 231) explaining the importance of human scale architecture, derived from the design of the open space that architecture contains and relates with. In this way architecture, articulating its contact range with the open space, intensifies the relation with human spirit and becomes a "substance of hoped things"[2].

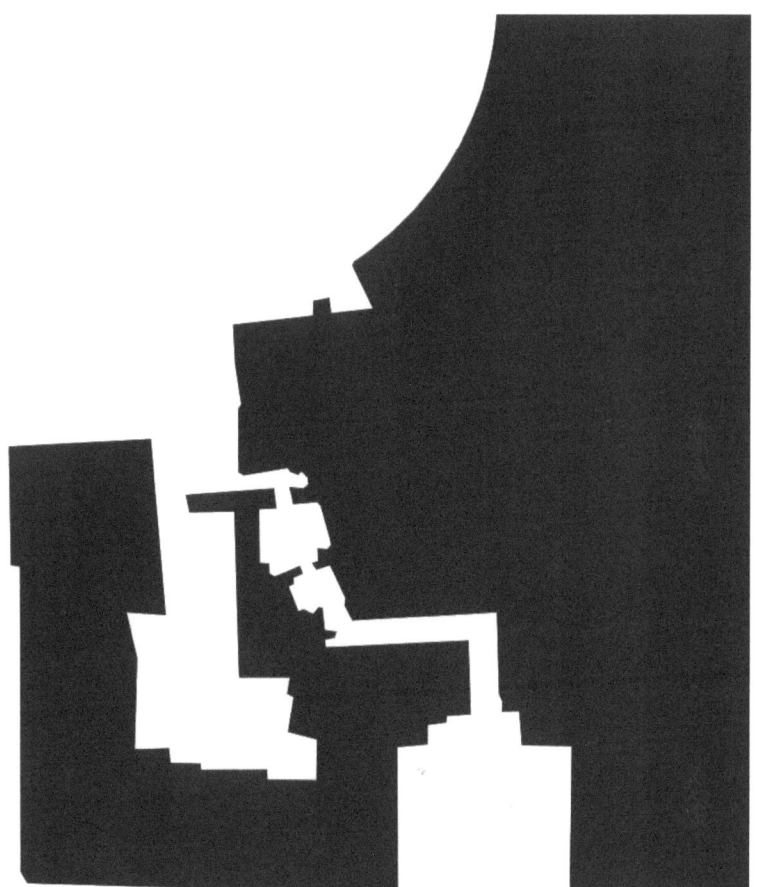

NOTES

[1] Espuelas F. 2016, "Il tempo della materia. Chronos versus Aiôn", in Maggiore, C. A. (a cura di), *Re-Use Ragusa. Strategie sostenibili per la rinascita del centro storico*, Mimesis, Milan, p. 61.

[2] Edoardo Persico, *Profezia dell'architettura*, conference held on 21/1/1935 in Turin.

BIBLIOGRAPHY

Biraghi M. 2017, *La sparizione dell'architettura*, http://www.gizmoweb.org/2017/07/la-sparizione-dellarchitettura/.

Chillida E. 2010, *Lo spazio e il limite*, Christian Marinotti Edizioni, Milano.

Espuelas F. 2004, *Il vuoto, riflessioni sullo spazio in architettura*, Christian Marinotti Edizioni, Milano.

Maggiore, C. A. (a cura di) 2016, *Re-Use Ragusa. Strategie sostenibili per la rinascita del centro storico*, Mimesis, Milano.

IMAGES

1. L'Atlàntida, J. Llinás, Vic (2010).jpg

2. Sant Antoni-Joan Oliver Library, RCR Arquitectes, Barcelona (2007).jpg

3. Archaeological area, R. Moneo, Cartagena (2008).jpg

All images are original artworks of the author.

Blurred Cities
Few words about unconscious waste of form

Carlalberto Amadori

Author Bio

Carlalberto Amadori
Licensed architect - Urbino and Milan.
PhD candidate at Faculty of Architecture in Florence.

Teaching assistant at Politecnico di Milano for the Design Studio II lead by professor Architect C.A. Maggiore. During 2016-17 he has been teaching assistant at Politecnico di Milano for Degli Esposti design studio I.
Visiting lecturer at Faculty of Architecture in Ferrara, October 2017.
Master of Science graduated with honor at Politecnico di Milano in 2017.

He worked in Spain, for RCR Arquitectes.
During 2016 he worked for Giancarlo De Carlo Architetti in Milan and Urbino.
He collaborated with Francesco Librizzi studio and Matilde Cassani for the 2013 Triennale Design Museum in Milan.

He's member and founder partner of Ground Action, a multidisciplinary collective. He is a part of the Landworks Plus staff; project winner of Culturability and 2018 Year of European Cultural Heritage.

The history of the city is the story of different forms of organization of the space, in political, economical and social meaning.

There is no City, but cities only.
The greek pòlis (from which it derives the word politic) is not the roman urbs (from which, urbanism), not even the civitas (from which, city). The medieval mediterranean city is not the baroque one; the modern city is not the contemporary metropolis, which is not the city where we're living nowadays.

The word *Contemporary*[1] clearly shows the necessity to contain all the times in the same time and space. Therefore the city itself is a changeable and contradictory reality, *a truth in the making*, it's a blurred and momentary appearance of stratification of sounds, wishes and desires.

The *mediterranean city* is anti-classical, it doesn't apply to any ideal scheme, it increases as it's used, in the temporal determination of its own functions. The *modern city* constitutes a violent overcoming which is based on the imposition on the *space-time* of the medieval city an *order*[2] founded on the synergy between factory and market, between production and consumption (of the spaces).

The time of the relation *production/consumption* regulates all the times and all the spaces.

We can call this phenomenon who spreads on every function and every aspect of collective life, *"hypnotic attraction"*. The modern city, in its evolution, radiates from its center, overwhelming every ancient persistence.
Its settlements become cases of the radiating system, along the central suburban axes. This *phenomenon* appears irreversible at a certain point: the physical expansion becomes even more occasional, less and less planned and governable. The more the *"nervous network"* devours the surrounding territory, the more its spirit seems to be lost; the less it seems able to order and rationalize the life that takes place there, its own image is out of control. All the powers are increasingly struggling to *territorialize*, at least to create forms of coexistence that are observable on the territory.

The necessity of a limit

Today's cities are constantly losing their symbolic value in favor of temporary representations of capital. We're assisting to the development of a city without a destination. Sometimes the city expands by request of the finances, sometimes decreases; the project itself becomes a currency of exchange.
The territory no longer knows any *nòmos*[3] , the necessary hierarchy of the limits has lost itself in the passage from the cities to the inhabited territories.

The global desire for *speed*, proximity to the centers of *commerce* and consumption, the need for a *communication* network, the will of the capital to make the offer more and more widespread, has made the city informal and dissolute, so that it can itself grow without any planning.

The *neoprimitive needs of consumption, network communication and self-representation* have become the new bulwarks of impulsive and compulsive development.
The image of the city, as well as the blurred image of the population who lives it, begins to lose definition. The idea that man was a *social animal* today clashes with the superabundance of images and with this, the desire to relate it to other individuals in society. The "society du spectacle" (Debord, 1967) stages temporary theaters of consumption, informal and apolitical, losing the deep, permanent and reassuring vision of the city.
The city is everywhere: therefore, there is no-City.

We no longer live in cities, but in territories.

The contemporary man refers his dwelling to regional dimension not to the *civitas* of origin founded on symbols and customs. The symbol becomes a tinsel of memory, the spatial scans are given by the road network, or urban infrastructure,

the monument, the iconographic values of the city give way to the publicity.

The possibility of setting boundaries defined to the city appears inconceivable, or rather, it has been reduced to a technical-administrative affair. We call *city* this area for absolutely occasional, perhaps economic, reasons. Its borders are nothing but a mere speculative artifice. The territory of post-urbanism is a geography of sporadic events, a putting into practice of connections and structures that cross "hybrid" landscapes.
The limit of contemporary urban space is only given by the boundary of the communications network, as the network becomes stronger we can move away from the city, post- metropolis but it is clear that it is a sui generis boundary: it exists only to be overcome, it's a tempo-

rary and random speculation.
This mental boundary is constantly in crisis.

The contemporary city is dissolute and blurred. The polarities in this space still exist. There are still activities which we can define as central, and which orientate forms of connection, mobility, etc. around us, we can recognize the islands of this archipelago and the memories of monuments, the strategic centers of the political life of the city, but we cannot delineate the figure, the form itself.
So the city is a territory that must be done, it appears but it does not exist in facts.

The truth as a form

The roles of center and periphery can be exchanged unceasingly and indistinctly on the basis of

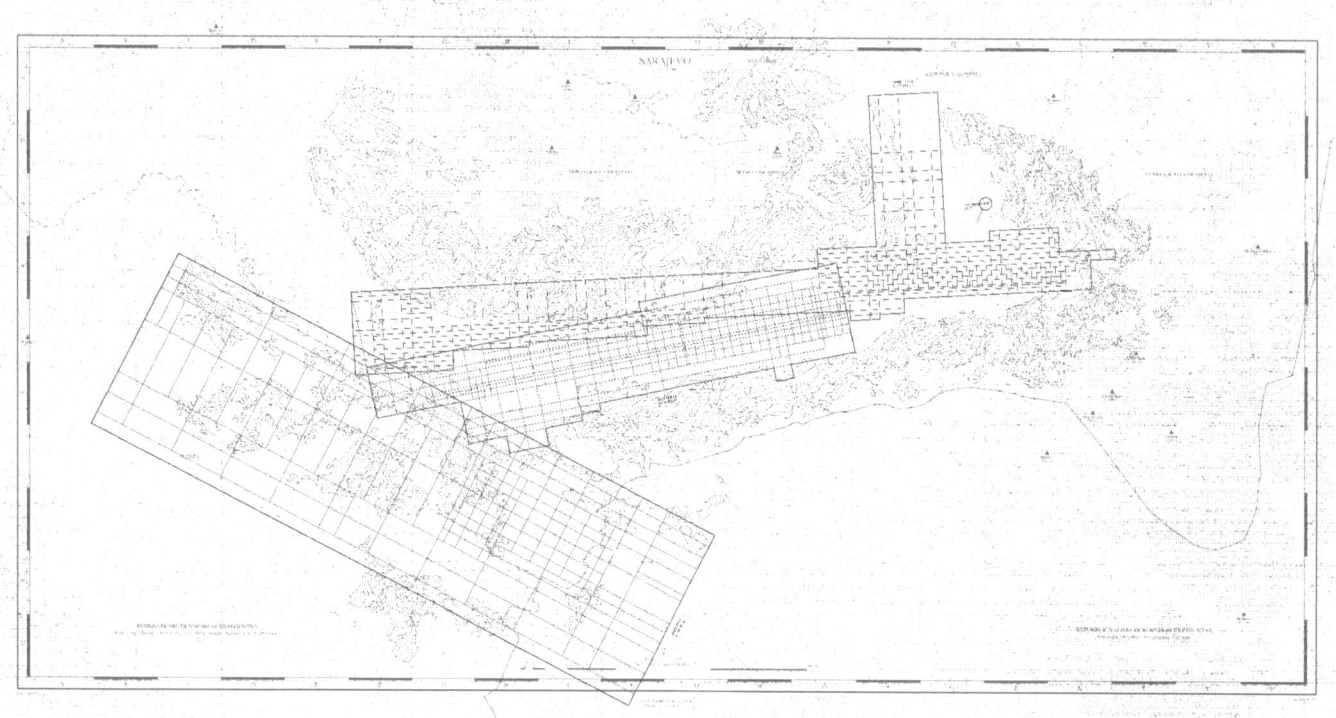

economic-social dynamics. All this happens on an occasional basis, or on the basis of mercantile and speculative logics, which reject any pre- constituted grid of functions or uses. The territory continues to specialize, outside of any overall project. It is the death of all the codifications of the Modern Movement, of its thinking of the city by parts, as a successive aggregation of elements, from the dwelling to the building, to the functional pole, to the whole city as container of containers. Is this the sunset of every abstract typology, or the opportunity to define something that is, but is not yet complete, the city to be? *La città in potenza*.

Life in the contemporary city is the end of every form of community, where the individual acts as a self-referenced singularity within a system devoid of social, spatial, urban references other than his own memory.

In other words, the territory of contemporaneity is the negation of the possibility of a single definable city; or can they ever invent places proper to the time when his life seems to have resolved itself?
We must face this philosophical and aesthetic paradox. The energy that emanates the territory of the contemporary city is essentially deterritorializing but at the same time we read of territory as an interconnected system of spaces in continuity "lieux où non lieux" (Augé, 1992). This same paradox makes the image of the city even more *contradictory*. Anti-spatial but unitary, isolated but interconnected, island and sea, archipelago among the emerged lands. Of course, we can affirm that the dynamic of disorientation had already begun with the modern metropolis, but today tends to express itself in its com-

pleteness. The loss of the formal boundaries, therefore of the truth of the form, entails the loss of the True.

"Ut ergo veritas forma verorum est, ita similitudo forma similium est". (Sant'Agostino)

The contradictory process of the loss of the formal boundaries of the city, the dissolution of the historical center, the proliferation of distributed identities, make the urban condition prerogative of an ambiguous vision between territory and landscape, between urbs and suburbs, ever less readable. The contemporary city is therefore the compromise between the ambiguities of social processes and the contradictions of form, between dilatation and implosion, between sprawl and shrink.

NOTES

[1] from latin cum-tempore: "with all the times".
[2] which is an form a priori
[3] Nomos, from ancient greek:"the Law" means at the origin, subdivision, articulation of a territory.

BIBLIOGRAPHY

Dogo, M., Pitassio, A. 2008, Città dei Balcani, città d'Europa. Studi sullo sviluppo urbano delle capitali post-ottomane, Argo, Lecce.

Andric I. 1993 , Racconti di Sarajevo, Newton Compton Editore, Roma.

Belpoliti M. 2014, L'età dell'estremismo, Guanda, Parma.

Greble E. 2012, Sarajevo la cosmopolita. Mussulmani, ebrei e cristiani nell'Europa di Hitler, Giangiacomo Feltrinelli Editore, Milano.

Foucault M. 2005, Sicurezza Territorio Popolazione, corso al College de France 1977-1979, Feltrinelli, Milano .

Rossi A. 1966 , L'architettura della città, Marsilio Padova.

Tafuri M. 1973 , Progetto e utopia, Laterza, Bari.

Maze H. 2006, Città e memoria. Beirut, Berlino, Sarajevo, Bruno Mondadori, Milano.

Cacciari M. 1994 , Geofilosofia dell'Europa; Adelphi, Milano.

Augè M. 2004, Rovine e Macerie, Bollat Boringhieri, Torino .

IMAGES

1. "The form of the politics", Urban mapping of Sarajevo, 2017. Glitch elaboration on digital map, Carlalberto Amadori

2. "Blurred", The shape of the city. Sarajevo 2017. Glitch elaboration on digital photography, Carlalberto Amadori

Eyes mirror of soul
How world discovers itself

Fabrizio Ferraro

Architecture has never been so complex and contradictory as today (Venturi 1993). Unique styles are no more needed to convey messages, in fact messages themselves are far from univocal due to technological development, globalization, plurality of information and real time exchange affecting every aspect of today life (De Fusco 2009, p. 320). Because of that, sometimes architecture itself fails to communicate, or even understand, the complex message of contemporaneity: more and more often we witness architecture attempts to embody multiple meanings ending up in emptiness and lack of any identity, infinitely reiterating undetermined forms (Augé 2009). Lacks in planning, building speculation, urban voids/interstices and landscape aberrations are just some examples of this phenomenon, whether they are legacy of the past or still in the process of becoming. All this is clearly in contrast with the concept of "Forma Urbis", which associates identity and meaning of the city to methodical form, making us think about the strategies we'll have to apply in the near future in order to get them back. What are order and form though, and why do we consider them necessary in order to define an object, an identity?

To answer this, we can elaborate the very definition of "order". This word comes directly from the latin term [ōrdo, ōrdĭnis] and means row, "regular arrangement of several things placed one after another according to an organic and reasoned principle, responding to purposes of convenience, suitability and harmony" (Treccani 2018). First of all it implies the existence of a geometric or spatial rule, or rather a method, in the disposition of one or more elements. Thus, the concept of order assumes the meaning of "manner", a rule in the state of things, not necessarily strict as long as explicable, which grants coherence and therefore sense, so that now the link between order and identity comes more clear: the existence of a rule guarantees meaning and allows the definition of the object itself, which is self-determined by its own ordered, oriented nature. From these assumptions we can easily deduce the concept of disorder, defined as a lack of logic and identity, one or more objects without mutual coherence and orientation, devoid of their "manner." At this point, however, we could ask ourselves: is it always possible to find an ordering principle in things in order to define them, starting from chaos?

Attempting to establish order, two opposed approaches can roughly be distinguished basing on method and outcome: one destructive or substitutive, the other conservative or critical. Although in the first case, according to the principle of tabula rasa, the drastic removal of the chaotic element and the consequent creation of a renewed order seems the

best choice on logical and sometimes executive level, it is also true that this kind of method results in a total loss of the original element and doesn't get along with the essential principle of adaptation. On the contrary, acting according to a strategy of conservation and analysis, chaos itself can often be able to generate its identity by itself following a process that, unlike the previous one in which the action of external forces is needed, starts from the inside, not smoothing but rather exposing contradictions implied in disorder itself and trying to find a counterpart to balance them, almost as in front of a mirror. And it is precisely the mirror, ultimate splitter and creator of counterparts, that will help us understand the paradox of form/identity, as Carroll (1989) did in his famous Through the Looking-Glass, and What Alice Found There: whichever the object in front of a mirror, it stands in front of its equal and opposite double, instantly establishing even a symmetrical relationship with it. As a creator of parallel universes, mirror legitimates whatever stands in front of him as the origin of what stands "on the other side", granting it not only conceptual and geometric meaning but also relational sense as part of a couple, although fictitious and not really existing.

This metaphor works well on the figurative level, however it certainly loses its effectiveness on the ontological one. In this sense the myth of Narcissus (Ovid 2015, book III, pp. 339-510), whose world is split into two just because of a specular representation, comes in our help. The original Narcissus stands in the world outside the mirror, the one in which free will exists, but feels meaningless, convinced of his inability to love anyone but himself; longing for his double inside the mirror, the one that on the contrary is in the world of denied possibilities and determinism, slave to what happens on the other side, Narcissus does nothing but try to deny the reality in which he is, that in which he feels he does not have a determination, thus ending up losing himself and his own humanity definitely. He does not understand that his realization and understanding passes through the love of the nymph Eco (through confrontation with the "other" in general) because he is lost in his reflection, in his empty icon, but above all because in such a situation of bewilderment he fails to fill his representation of a meaning, to understand and therefore to love himself: putting the whole sense of his existence in the contemplation of his own image,

he faces an irresolvable contradiction from which he comes out torn and unable to self identify. On the contrary, the reverse paradox happens to Calvino's Valdrada, a city built on the shores of a large lake, and to its twin sister: the two cities "live for each other, their eyes interlocked; but there is no love between them" (Calvino 1972, p.25). Here too, the original and its reflection mutually depend one another but end up in conflict: the city above has been built and lives in function of its continuous reflection of each gesture and element, a reflection which, however, gives back an image of the original which is not alive at all, prisoner in its own nature of double. With Narcissus we witness the disintegration of the original individuality in its incorporeal double, in Valdrada we find an image inevitably devalued by the same subject it must represent: in both cases the relationship of duality with the double can't legitimate alone the meaning of the subject on a metaphysical level (relative to sole existence, regardless of its concrete manifestations), being the rule that intends it subordinated and limited only to the visual, and therefore physical, level. (Perego 2003)

Where to reflect, then, when mirror is not capable to? Once again, this time in his Mr Palomar, Calvino (1990) helps us guess a possible answer: "But how can you look at

something and set your ego aside? Whose eyes are doing the look? As a rule, you think of the ego as one who is peering out of your own eyes as if leaning on a windowsill, looking at the world stretching out before him in all its immensity. So then: there is a window that looks out on the world. The world is out there; and in here, what is there? The world still — what else could there be? [...] and for the occasion has been split into a looking world and a world looked at. And what about him, also known as "I", namely Mr Palomar? Is he not a piece of the world looking at another piece of world? Or else, given that there is world that side of the window and world this side, perhaps the I, the ego, is simply the window through which the world looks at the world."

Therefore, if mirror constitutes a sill, an edge (Lynch 2001) between the dimension of reality and the unreal dimension of its opposite, on the contrary the eye (or rather the ego) constitutes the threshold between two real worlds, more precisely between two real parts of the same world which, according to an hegelian principle (Hegel 1995), doesn't need any mirror to reflect and reflect on its nature, since it always watches itself through its own eyes. Outer and inner research for order are thus revealed as faces of the same coin: the need for inner affirmation is projected to the

outside as a will to give an identity to the external world, at the same time contradictions of the external world are perceived as a reflection of the internal ones. The search for a form of the world, an order of things, is therefore nothing more than the search for ourselves, for the rule that gives us a sense, from the outside to the inside and from the inside to the outside.

Concluding, how can these last concepts help us in dealing with the "disordered city"? Perhaps, asking ourselves what of us resides in it and what of its face is actually part of us, we will not only be able to explain the sense of uneasiness it generates but also how to approach its unsolved situations. If it is true that the search for an external order corresponds to that of an in-

ner balance, it is also legitimate to think it is possible to interchange these two methods of research. Human being, by nature, is a creature which borns and remains imperfect but which tends to improve by turning to his own advantage the errors he commits, unable to cancel them; so, can the city, dwelling of man, follow a similar process of growth and improve itself accor-

ding to this principle? Trying to put such suggestion into practice, and not so unexpectedly, it seems clear that episodes of poor urbanization mentioned before constitute failures in the way of making cities only as long as we consider them as such: when the veil of mistake that surrounds them falls of and we begin to consider them from a critical point of view as objects that highlight critical issues, problems or needs, they transform into start points. In short, it is a matter of recognizing "urban errors" as human errors and acting accordingly, since the firsts are none other than the manifestation of the seconds. Concretely speaking: degraded environments, places lacking in identity, infrastructures now in disuse, can in fact constitute chances to understand the meaning of city and how man conceives it as a projection of himself. Not only that, these situations can and should be episodes of positive growth and enhancement of the city, opportunities for new projects designed to be cornerstones of a strategy based on recovery, renewal, reconversion and reuse, as if they were seams reuniting edges of (urban) tissues, consolidating the city of the present into that of the future.

BIBLIOGRAPHY

Augé M. 2009, Nonluoghi: introduzione a una antropologia della surmodernità (Non-Places, introduction to an anthropology of supermodernity), Elèuthera, Milan

Calvino I. 1972, Le città invisibili (Invisible cities), Einaudi, Turin

Calvino I. 1990, Palomar (Mr Palomar), Mondadori, Milan

Carroll L. 1989, Alice nel paese delle meraviglie - Attraverso lo specchio (Through the looking-glass, and what Alice found there), Garzanti, Milan

De Fusco R. 2009, Storia del Design, Laterza, Bari

Hegel GWF. 1995, Fenomenologia dello spirito (The phenomenology of spirit), Rusconi, Milan

Lynch K. 2001, L'immagine della città (The image of the city), Marsilio, Venice

Ovid 2015, Metamorfosi (Metamorphoses), Einaudi, Turin

Perego M. 2003, Specchi d'autore tra fiaba e realtà, http://www.lettere.unimi.it/Spazio_Filosofico/leparole/2003/mpspec.htm

Treccani G. 2018, Enciclopedia Italiana (english translation made by the author), Istituto dell'Enciclopedia Italiana, Rome

Venturi R. 1993, Complessità e contraddizioni nell'architettura (Complexity and contradiction in architecture), Dedalo, Bari

IMAGES

Original artworks by the author

Material Memory and collective memory
Permanence and continuity in the urban form

Cristian Sammarco

Author Bio

Graduated at the Faculty of Architecture "La Sapienza" of Rome in 2016 after an internship at the Proap studio of Joao Nunes (2013-2014), he entered the Draco PhD Program in Architecture and Construction at "La Sapienza" in November 2016 and carries out research on the theme of urban morphology. He participates in several international conferences such as ISUF Valencia and Italy and is part of the editorial office of urban U + D morphology magazine directed by professor Giuseppe Strappa. His research focuses on the relationship between the ancient city and the contemporary city and on the formative process of the urban fabric. Participates in numerous international workshops in India, Canada and Italy on the theme of design in the historic city. He is a teaching assistant in architectural design courses, urban morphology and interior architecture at "La Sapienza".

Understanding the built reality and the anthropized territory on which we want to act, is the first tool for designing an architectural form that is not atopic but interwoven with a telos already given. The architect has to work with a *materia signata* (Strappa 2014, p.51) a stratification of traces and permanences that are traceable and visible in the morphology of our cities. Who are the subjects of urban transformations? It is the fabric itself, intended as a synthetic organism. Through its paths and artifacts, it is at the same time product and material in every phase of the training process.

We are dealing with a canvas, which allows us to move without mistakes, without the fear of the blank sheet, interpreting and rewriting in a continuous cycle the forms that history gives us in every age. It is necessary to know how to read the underlying traces, the substratum, the shape that lies beneath, and which orients (re-emerging), the contemporary project giving continuity and organicity to the new buildings.

The schools of Italian architecture of the twentieth century have opened a great debate , still current, on the theme of memory and on the role of the past as an instrument for the project. Through the works of French geographers of the first half of the 20th century, Aldo Rossi gives us a "theory of permanences" in which the monument is collective memory, object as primary subject that represents the continuity of the urban form and the values of a community, over time and in society. According to Rossi, "knowledge of the past is the term of comparison and the measure of the future": the "urban facts", adhering to the thought of Marcel Poète find their reason for being in their continuity. A more or less apparent link is established between the forms through time. It adheres, in an interstitial way, to the relationships taken from Poète between the city and the geographical area; "The city is born in a given place but it is the road that keeps it alive. Associating the city's destiny with communication routes is therefore a fundamental rule of method ". And the road, or the path of man, his progress in space and time, the main plot of telòs (Rispoli 2016, p.25)

On the other hand, Carlo Aymonino, places the "physical" sign of a political power as the main substratum. It is the need to represent a way that unite the urban centers, in a specific place: "the city is therefore an artificial place of history in which every epoch, every society has come to diversify from the one that preceded it, tries, through the representation of itself in architectural monuments, the impossible: to mark "that" determined time, beyond the necessities and the contingent reasons for which the buildings were built " (Aymonino 2000, first chapter).

The idea of monument as a testimony of the substratum for Aymonino lies precisely in the denial of their eternal character, presupposed to their birth; everything changes and varies in historical - social time. The nature of eternity lies in the continuity of their physical presence. The "meaning of the city" lies in the transition from unity, from the monument as a singular fact, to the city as a monument. In the baroque Rome that " summarizes and burns" the previous substrates in a new city, there is the most virtuous example of reorganization of partial references in an organic whole.

Rome is the subject of studies for Saverio Muratori in the search for an identification of a method of reading the contemporary city through a Heghelian concept of "working history" (Muratori S. 1963, p.11). In the tissues of the eternal city it is possible to recognize an "organic hierarchy of forms", whose object of study is not the value of the single event represented by the monument but the minor construction: the residential building from which the events emerge predominant. As Gianfranco Caniggia then affirms, it is the house, and its settlement and aggregation process, that represent the collective memory in a cyclic return of forms. Muratori states that it is possible to recognize the permanence of building types and functional and structural characters which, compared to linguistics, represents the grammar with which to compose not only prose but also poetry; or the monument. In Rome it is possible to study the whole range of possible structures and their training processes: Rome is the city of memory par excellence, which contracts and expands, re-establishing itself. It is the clarity and synthesis of the formative

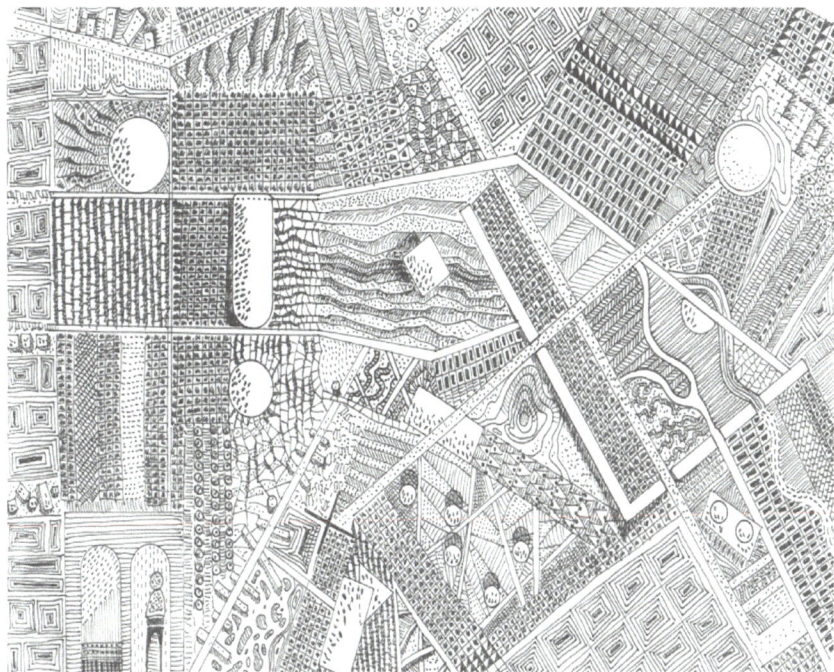

process of the tissues to represent in every epoch the memory of what was (the materia signata), of what is (the visible form), and of what will be (the material). In Rome the memory of monuments as a permanence, tangible trace, is deprived of its original functional value to become material, to become home. This is the case of the great ancient cohesive structures such as theaters, odeon, circuses, which lose their monument value but not of memory. In the Middle Ages, the cryptae, an anthropic and prototype form, are inserted between their arches, and the terraced houses which, through the re-casting of special organisms such as the palaces, become monuments again. The ruins of these large architectural complexes are both evidence of the decay and material and structure for a future construction site. Stays as well as physical ones are also intangible, like the memory of a Locus through oral tradition , flanked by a dimensional immateriality that completes the meaning of collective memory. We must make architecture sing and speak, as Paul Valéry wrote, in its historical environment to guarantee its consistency and continuity. Speaking is the transmission of the Tipo, whose debate seems to have turned off in the last twenty years, and that the authors cited considered fundamental for the transmissibility of the form.

Aldo Rossi wrote: "I think of the concept of type, are a problem of permanent and complex, a logical statement that is before form and that matter" (Rossi 2011, p.31) His vision came from the study of Quincy's thought that the "did not represent the image of something to be copied, but the idea of an element that concerns him, an abstract platonic conception.

For Aymonino, on the other hand, the building type returns to reckon with the political power and hierarchical organization of society: this results in a superstructure imposed by a hegemonic class that changes to the change in the structure of class relations.

The Muratorian school instead accepts, as already mentioned, the Heghelian concept, meaning the type as "first synthesis " (Caniggia 1997, p. 49) whose result is a direct contact with the built reality and with the formative process that transmits the memory of the urban form through its cycles. historical, economic and political.

Today we experience a moment of architectural crisis as we underestimate memory and history. We do not mean our products as a continuation of the reality in which we want to insert them. If we look at the cities of today we find the cities of yesterday, sometimes hidden in a synthesis so marvelous as to appear "new objects". The masters of the past shaped the material respectful of its nature, of its potential to be material for a new process. Michelangelo did not design the Piazza del Campidoglio having to do with an empty work plan, free from constraints. He had material permanencies, testimonies of the substrates that had taken place in the most important civil site in Rome. His genius was in understanding that he had to synthesize all the transformations, which had to crystallize the memory of the place in a new organism that could contain all the past urban events. Michelangelo, had to do with a medieval senatorial palace built on the structures of the ancient Roman tabularium that was to be the background, the visible memory of the project scene. He exploited the non-orthogonality of the other building present, less than the senatorial palace, doubling it symmetrically with respect to the axis of the square. It gave rise to a perspective effect which, together with the statue and the system of ascent paths, is the antecedent of the type of baroque theater (Purini 2017, p.37) The new material, the new architectural project, is born by transforming the material we have. The material memory must be consumed to be reconverted, but must be questioned; in fact, the present and the city can answer our questions through careful reading.

NOTES

[1] An interesting anthology of writings that reconstruct the schools of Italian thought is "tipologia architettonica e morfologia urbana. Il dibattito italiano – antologia 1960-1980" edited by Michele Caja, Martina Landsberger and Silvia Malcovati;

[2] Toponosmastics has transmitted the identity of many places and monuments through time, as stated by Capoferro Cencetti in Variazioni nel tempo dell'identita' funzionale di un monumento: il teatro di Pompeo, Bretschneider, 1979;

[3] Caniggia in "Ragionamenti di Tipologia" affirms that the concept of home is to be considered equal and different from the previous one.

BIBLIOGRAPHY

Aymonino C. 2000, Il significato delle città, Marsilio, Venezia.

Caniggia G. 1977, Ragionamenti di Tipologia. Operatività della tipologia processuale in architettura, Alinea, Firenze.

Muratori S. et al. 1963, Studi per una operante storia urbana di Roma, C.N.R., Roma.

Gurrieri, F. 2017 (a cura di) Purini, F., La storia e il nuovo, in Architettura contemporanea e Ambiente storico, Angelo Pontercorboli Editore, Firenze.

Rispoli, F. 2016, Forma Data e Forma Trovata. Interpretare/progettare l'architettura, Istituto Italiano per gli Studi Filosofici, Napoli.

Rossi A. 2011, L'Architettura della città, Quodlibet, Macerata.

Strappa G. 2014, L'Architettura come Processo: il mondo plastico murario in divenire, Franco Angeli, Roma.

IMAGES

1. Sammarco C., Geometrie di permanenza, china on paper, 2018

2. Photo of the occluded arcades of the theater of Marcello, Rome, beginning of the 20th century. Public Domain

3. The theater of Marcello in a view of the Piranesi, note the terraced houses and the Orsini palace. Public Domain

City whispers
Three projects talking about city

Letizia Gorgo, M.Sc.

Author Bio

Letizia Gorgo is a 29 years old architect. She studied at the University of Rome Sapienza where she graduated in 2014. She has a postgraduate degree in Applied architecture, at March, Fran Silvestre Arquitectos, Valencia, Spain, Universidad Europea de Madrid. She is Phd student at University of Rome Sapienza, focusing her studies in architectural research on space, its conformation, in relation to people activities. Her interest are also to the city and the relationship between urban development and architectural activity

The contemporary city doesn't need superb feats, amazing moments or radical turning points. The necessity resides in modest yet courageous interventions which do not have to insist on a denotative level, instead they have to voice and try to make sense to a connotative meaning.

It would be more therapeutical comparing the whisper of tradition to the desperate shout of the innovation.

The city here is intended as manmade matter, a cultural manifestation of social life, as an ensemble of elements so that a man adapts them to the environment and organizes his own social life. (Dei 2012, p.20) Anthropologist Richard Bauman concedes an univocal interpretation of those aspects (tradition and social life), giving his definition of tradition: "social need to give a meaning to our lives linking us to a significant past" (Bauman 1992, p.92). So we have to put into our personal database the meaning of "city" and of "tradition", translated also as the "spatial matrix of architecture".

Trying to connect parts and raw concepts ideally defined, Espuelas introduces Void as a spatial category: "Primary category tasked with obtain a space in favor of man" (Espuelas), him too pertaining to the social dimension of architecture.

Summing up: tradition, social life and voids are elements which should drive, albeit on an ideal level,

the city's change therefore acting as beacons for contemporary architecture. By fully entering into the architectonic experience, it should be noted how perceived void assumes a significance important as the role of architecture in the city. For that purpose we analyze an apparatus, a membrane (diaframma): the portico. Why the portico? Because here lies and begins the "matter deprivation" experience.

As in every significant experience there's a beginning and an end, that allows us to comprehend what we have just left (the ante-beginning principle), meanwhile the post-beginning lets us savor what we will partake in the shortly thereafter. This is what happens in the portico experience. Piazza San Marco comes to mind as an abused image by architects given its spectacularity. We should not focus on the church's triumphant presence or the shadows generated by the belfry, we should not focus on the colors or the church's image itself. We have to focus just on the transition between the "narrow" city, made of canals, of blind and pokey calle and to the blank space in the Piazza covered by the sky, with a stunning turn of events. The transition is smoothed by the portici which encircle three sides of the void, letting us understand the changing of the city narrative. From a shadow-predominant situation we pass into semi-darkness to end up trough a dazzling light. It's possible not recognising immediately to the void but it manifest itself while traversing the portico and basking in constant semi-darkness, while living the path as a manifestation of time and space. The portico is a staple of mediterranean cities, so that naturally it delineates the scope of our investigation.

Through three types of architecture, of a different time and place, it happens the exploration of this vibrant transitional space.

The Aldo Rossi's Gallaratese residential intervention (1969-1973) around Monte Amiata presents a similar experience to the Venetian one. The "blade" that integrates into Aymonino's plan has a ground connection that presents the portico's path as a transitory element between the cut, represented by the building and the square in front, rather than being categorically portrayed in a simple planimetric layout.

The Roman experience, that preceded the Milanese one, pertains the Villaggio Olimpico (1954 project). The transitional situation here is the "spread" over the intervention area; there are multiple paths and the experience is based on the void which goes with the "piano pilotis". In fact Piazza Grecia is a valley compared to the project's orography, with 4 main access points on the 4 sides, 2 of which include the transition "filter". It's really a double filter though: in fact coming from Piazza

Palach we pass through a semi-darkness area, traversing the building's piano pilotis which encircles the void to the east and then we traverse another "thickness", the one interrupting the commercial floor on Piazza Grecia, reaching in the end the "greek light".

In this project the size of the void is significant, reflecting the social character of the intervention. If the experience just illustrated winks at the highest level of community, everything is seen through a domestic len compared to le Crocette di Libera. Here everything revolves around a private dimension: passing the public void of the street we enter into the penumbra of the space that lies between public and private areas, where the meaning between "built and empty" is in a precarious balance. The path here is interesting because it does not occur solely on an horizontal level, but has also a vertical nature. This hybrid vertical dimension carries on to the walkways leading up to the individual flats, multiplying the experience along the Y axis.

Changing coordinates

In Evora, Portugal, the architect Alvaro Siza in 1977 projected the intervention, of an urbanistic-residential area giving birth to a new quad. Surpassing the typical narrative of the residential building, the idea is that tradition activates inno-vation between the city. A strong character of the architecture mentioned above, resides in a perimeter wall (muro di cinta), delimiting the project and making it an historical promenade. The intervention on urban scale follows several axis, every one of which owns a "head", that it is easily associated to a sign representing an ancient Roman aqueduct. From this sign the intervention begins, and it's right there where the passage delimits the before and after. Even in this case the path is doubled, in fact the transition happens twice: at ground level on the quarter development axis and on the higher level along the path of the "blade".

"The creation that links a space and the person who occupies it defines the place itself and the experience which other people have in a priva-te setting. Space and occupant put together a natural unity that loses merit when the occupant is absent. An observer, in this circumstance, perceiving the frustration of his expectations, objectifies the place as a void" (Espuelas, p.203)

The city, social reactivity and the void

The murmuring of architecture should participate to relational and spatial policies. Void becomes substance of the city-building architecture and the city itself becomes an habitat of actions and relationships between its inhabitants. In a reality dominated by icons, the "absence", the void, can make a strong impression. With "absence" we do not mean a lack of something, a non-intervention. In the contemporary world, full of slogans, of forms, of quick gestures that progressively lose sense, we like to imagine absence as a "conventional gesture": in a world that sells nonconventional in every field, the conventional becomes the anti-nonconventional.

Here's why for this dissertation we chose three projects that operate in an extreme simplicity: a square, where its actual conformation is the outcome of centuries of historical changes; a residential building, as a domestic meeting, a shared space and a planned working-class quarter, where spaces for public and private life are being shaped as an ensemble.

The key of interpretation is a "device" that summarizes these three different situations, a physical element that while losing its substance becomes a logical device of approach and transition, avoiding sudden changes as in the natural evolution, between light and shadow.

BIBLIOGRAPHY

Espuelas F. 2004, il vuoto: riflessioni sullo spazio in architettura, Marinotti, Milano.

Dei F. 2012, Antropologia culturale, il Mulino, Bologna.

Baumann Z. 1992, Intimations of Postmodernity, Psychology press, London.

IMAGE
Quartiere Flaminio, Roma: https://it.wikipedia.org/wiki/File:Roma_Stadio_Flaminio_-_Villaggio_Olimpico_-_Ponte_Milvio.jpg,
Public domain

REPORTAGE

Through amnesia
Artistic interventions in spaces of oblivion

Enrica Corvino

Author Bio

Enrica Corvino (Lecce, 1986) is an architect with a PhD in Architectural and Urban Design (Architecture and Design Department – La Sapienza University of Rome, 2017). She works as a teaching assistant and researcher. Since 2013 she also works at an architecture firm as an assistant. She has published various essays and was editor of the volume La modernità delle rovine ("The Modernity of Ruins"), published by Prospettive Edizioni in 2015.

"Emptiness is an endless resource to cross. It grants unexpected possibilities, offers itself to utopian projections, inspires unexpected and unimaginable questions. […] Empty spaces constantly arise questions without answers."

Francesco Careri

French philosopher Henri Bergson describes memory as an actual non-place in his 1886 work *Matter and Memory. Essay on the relation of body and spirit*. Memory is an elsewhere space that shrouds the present at all times, but that belongs to a sort of other dimension. Parallel to memory, the world of oblivion emerges, a world made up of forgotten things. Memory is oblivion and oblivion is memory. They're not opposing antagonists, but complementary, necessarily connected (Castelli Gattinara, 2001, pp. 149-158). Memory is the building block of urban narration and design, and remembering in itself is a design choice: we choose what to remember, what to emphasize.

But how can we give meaning to such forgotten places, to spaces of oblivion left over by the city's urban evolution?

Empty space is suitable for exploration, investigation, crossing, and to be walked in. The act itself of crossing it, "*a simultaneously perceiving and creative act*"(Careri, 2006, p.16), gives it meaning. It is, however, a difficult space to categorize, elusive and ever-changing as it is.

Urban strategies seem to lack the power or the interest in doing something about the rejected and cast-off. On the other hand, artistic experimentation gives enlightening contributions on re-appropriation and the birth of a new awareness of a place, on the definition and re-interpretation of these amnesia spaces in the urban texture. In these cases, art

"can be an instrument to re-awaken the people's awareness and critical spirit, to inspire creativity and the ability to generate something original; a language of cultural mediation built on exclusive syntax and an interdisciplinary lexicon." (Seta, 2011, p.50)

A good example of this is Edward Ruscha's *Thirty-four parking lots in Los Angeles*, a photographic investigation of the open-air parking lots of the city in the sixties. The result is an atlas of empty places, documented by the artist to underline the value given by repetitiveness. Elevated to typology, these unintended empty spaces become intervals and fragments, by now absorbed and embedded in the urban experience. (Marini, 2014, p.75)

In the same vein, the work of Gordon Matta Clark on residual spaces and non-places appears as a sort of abacus of underused space. The project, titled *Reality properties: fake estates*, started in 1973, when New York auctioned off some small residual areas that had eluded the attention of real estate, at a price between 25 and 75 dollars each. The artist bought some, and started to document them with photographs and measurements. These spaces were considered invisible not because they were hard to access (although some were), but because they didn't have any viable use.

The intent of the work was to document the city's irrationality, to use these *anomalies* to reveal the contradictions of urban growth and economical development. In the city that expands without limits, such discarded spaces aren't on the borders with the countryside anymore, but inside the urban texture. They become places of marginalization.

The city's residues pass from one inappropriate function to the next, or stay suspended in the limbo of absence. Sometimes they go back to previous configurations, other times they are subject to irreversible change. Their invisible palimpsest becomes part of the city's stratification.

Only the artistic intervention can change the paradigm inside such places, modifying the perception (or its absence) society has of them and its relevancy in the urban structure.

As Marcel Duchamp said,

"All in all, the creative act is not performed by the artist alone; the spectator brings the work in contact with the external world by de-

ciphering and interpreting its inner qualifications and thus adds his contribution to the creative act".

Relational art is based on this concept; its "theoretical and pragmatic starting point is the web of human relations and their social context, instead of an autonomous and restrictive space" (Bourriad, 2010, p.105). The works of relational artists generate interpersonal meetings. Their effect is dependent on the participation of the public. It's an interesting approach when imagined as transposed on the urban scale, where the artistic piece in itself isn't that important – the meeting it generates between different realities is. What matters is the process to reach that piece, the re-activation of the forgotten place it inhabits.

"Sherit is the leftover, reshit is the beginning, two distant words in English but united in that language [Hebrew - author's note] by the mysterious bond of the anagram. […] Maybe it's possible to withstand being a residue, unjustified and unauthorized to the world, only if one believes in the impossible design that uses being a residue as building block of a beginning" (Clemente, 2015, p.83)

BILIOGRAPHY

Castelli Gattinara E. 2001, Il non luogo della memoria e dell'oblio, in «Aperture», n.10 , pp. 149-158.

Careri F. 2006, Walkscapes. Camminare come pratica estetica, Einaudi, Torino.

Seta C. 2011, Paesaggio con figura, in Sardi G. (edited by), «Paesaggio con figura. Arte, sfera pubblica e trasformazione sociale», U. Allemandi & C., Torino.

Marini S. 2014, Cataloghi di realtà. L'architettura del territorio inverso, in Pavia R., Secchi R., Gasparrini C. (edited by) «Il territorio degli scarti e dei rifiuti», Aracne, Roma,

Duchamp M. 1957, Intervento alla Convention of the American Federation of Arts, Houston, Texas, 3-6 aprile 1957. Published in «Art News», vol 56, n.4.

Bourriaud N. 2010, Estetica relazionale, Postmediabooks, Milano.

Clemente A. A. 2015, Il resto come principio, in Quaderni del PRIN 08 «Re-cycle Italy. Il territorio degli scarti e dei rifiuti», Aracne, Roma.

IMAGES

1. Kurt Perschke, RedBall Project Lausanne, 8 July 2013, 16:13:59, Source: Own work, Author: Redballproject, Creative Commons Attribution-Share Alike 3.0 Unported license. https://commons.wikimedia.org/wiki/File:RedBall_Project_Lausanne.jpg

2. Français : Art urbain de Julien Malland dit "Seth" sur le belvédère au parc de Belleville (20e arrondissement de Paris), December 2014, Source: http://www.street-art-avenue.com/2015/01/seth-parc-de-belleville-paris-10494, Author: Julien SETH, Malland / Parc de Belleville Paris – déc 2014 @vidos / street-art-avenue, Creative Commons Attribution 3.0 Unported license. https://commons.wikimedia.org/wiki/File:Street-art-avenue-julien-seth-malland-paris-belleville_24-574x800.jpg

3. Français : Art urbain de Julien Malland dit "Seth" sur le belvédère au parc de Belleville (20e arrondissement de Paris). Vue d'ensemble, December 2014, Source: http://www.street-art-avenue.com/2015/01/seth-parc-de-belleville-paris-10494, Author: Julien SETH Malland / Parc de Belleville Paris – déc 2014 @vidos / street-art-avenue. Creative Commons Attribution 3.0 Unported license. https://commons.wikimedia.org/wiki/File:Street-art-avenue-julien-seth-malland-paris-belleville_26-678x381.jpg

4. E. Corvino, Incompiuto/ritrovato, Lago Sandro Pertini, Ex Snia Viscosa, Roma. 2016.

Bari
I searched for the city

Michela Ronco

Author Bio

Michela Ronco was born near Turin, Italy, in 1989, She graduated in Architecture at the Turin Politecnico, with a thesis consisting of photographic documentation of the Ionic coast landscape in the Calabria region. She then completed the Master Course in contemporary image provided by the Fondazione Fotografia Modena, academic years 2015/2017. She is interested in capturing urban landscapes, using an architectural language to discuss contemporary themes such as migrations, inhabiting spaces or the stiffness of architectural design

I inspected Bari urban planning and how this affects the way people experience the city. This project started from the Libertà area, a neighbourhood that was completed when the expansion of the city beyond the railway line was already well under way. The area is defined as peri-central just for its position, as for what concerns its morphology, it is located considerably close to the city centre, while presenting typical problems and features of Italian outskirts.

The grid plan blocks are regularly laid out in the Libertà area. On the first days at the job, I tried and look for reference points on which base my work; then, I thoroughly covered the neighbourhood confines: east, the border is not defined well near the Murat area, whereas Corso Vittorio Veneto and the port delimit it north. Via Brigata Regina is located west, while the railway line and Corso Italia south. These last two places made me feel as if I could not go forward, as if the passage was blocked. In my search for such elements that instilled the perception of limitation, I came across some specific venues that not only gave me an insight of the area through its flows, but also embodied perfectly the sensations that Bari triggered in me as a city, strolling around and living in it.

The photography project is composed of sights articulated in diptychs or triptychs to allow the observer to have a bigger picture of these spaces, to think about the movement. Not only is the photo used as a survey tool, it is also part of a gestural, behavioural attitude that changes depending on the situation, to allow the observer to switch its gaze and perceptions. This was the criterion chosen for the case of via Brigata Regina. These three pictures reveal the intersection of three different road axes that create a sort of movement, rather than an overview. Heading toward the motorway, the road becomes underpass Giuseppe Filippo. At street level, there is the passage to the Brigata railroad station, which shares access to the raised tube you can glimpse in a few photos. Very important road is Brigata Regina street, one of the main road-vehicle axes of the city that leads to the port, from land to sea.

The first two photos were taken around the Japigia area. The Giuseppe Garibaldi bridge crosses the railway in the vicinity of the swimming beaches called Bread and Tomato. The next two photographs concern the Luigi di Savoia underpass, where you can get a glimpse of a comparison between buildings belonging to different periods: the main bridge loses its marble façade, hidden behind the flyover connecting via Dieta di Bari, a maintenance work aimed at facilitating car traffic and avoiding the crossroad.

Inside the Libertà area, there are not many public spaces. We have the Courthouse and the Renaissence Square, that is one of the few structures that were object of urban restructuring works. What is very important is the area occupied by the former ManufactureTabacchi, which now hosts the market. The

Apulian government is expected to redevelop this complex with a research centre, called "innovation factory".

The area placed next to the cemetery is emblematic. Located outside the walls of the nineteenth-century city, in my opinion, the area means to relate with the modern bridge, the Adriatico bridge, which was open to public in January 2017, with the purpose of relieving traffic congestion from and to the port and from the Fiera del Levante (tradeshow) in Brigata Regina street.

Not only do these places mark borders and limits, but also state clearly the bond of the contemporary metropolitan city, which flanks the still-alive city that was conceived initially and shows itself in its most functional way. Think of this concept as weaves of the urban fabric, which reveal sides of the city we are not really willing to define as identity-making.

Try to picture you portraying the city of Bari. We do not depict "its landscape" using only our eyes but by walking around it, experiencing it step by step. I think the approach to the contemporary landscape depends on sensitivity, the permeability to anything surrounding us and embracing our living.

49

Lucubration and hypochondria
Anamorphic scenarios of the city

Antonella Pettorruso, M.Sc.

Author Bio

Antonella Pettorruso was born in Venosa, the city of Horace, on 1st January 1991. Since childhood and adolescence, she is interested in the art world, building creative objects with cardboard and dedicating to reading and poetry. She attended the Classical High School Q.Orazio in Lavello, her hometown, where she lived up to the age of 19, when she moved to Turin to attend the Architecture course at the Politecnico di Torino. During the university years among exams and workshops, she cultivates the passion for research and design, achieving the graduation with 108/110 on the 19 December 2017. Now, she is Ph.D. student in Architectural and Landscape Haritage at the Politecnico di Torino. Thanks to this study, Antonella discovers a strong interest in the "artwork as incomplete object". Other than the research activity, she carries out the professional practice at the Studio Vertice in Lavello and in the leisure time she is dedicated to art, graphical, design and poetry contest.

The text does not aim to solve the problem of contemporary cities' limits scenarios' contraposition. In fact, firstly it will be analysed the elements of the "the dream of sustainability", successively the "nightmare of global warming".

Nowadays, the word sustainability is cumbersome, overestimated for its potential and overburden of interdisciplinary meanings. For this reason, the metropolis are "obliged" to improve, researching microsurgery's interventions, considerable out of scale compared to the city's dimension.

Like a recipe, we can find the "ingredients" of the sustainable urban transformation: square meters of planting (better if autochthonous) in order to improve the air quality, kilometres of cycle path road surfaces to limit car emissions or kilograms of turf to cover flat roofs and turn them into green roofs.

Do these interventions really improve our metropolis? Maybe are these elements more and more crushed by the elements of the "unsustainable city" system? May we really believe that factories can be eliminated and that it can be possible to go back to self-handling and bartering? A business traveller can really think to use only "sustainable transportation" to travel from Milan to Rome every day?

The drift between dream and nightmare are moving away the architects, the urban planners, the responsible of res-publica and the metro-polis from the "patient research" of the effective solution for the change. The result of this incorrect research is changing the way the human being is approaching to nature and his habitat's construction.

The climate warming will bring to build underground cities to deal with the extreme high temperatures. The idea of the "green invasion" will aim to build "tree houses". All of these is more and more oriented to produce "yes-buildings", i.e. highly performing, super technological and able to store data to improve their performance.

Thinking at the change of the cities, the architecture and their adaptation to different conditions, it has always been a complex problem. However, it has been produced positive solutions, only if free from the Promethean architect's figure. It is referring to the choral design of vernacular architecture of the cities constructed on the territory's morphological traces.

The error of the sustainable utopia relies on thinking that everything is solvable through the delivery of critical data to the world of numbers, even though the project and the city's transformation has always been connected to the image as its representation.

To delegitimize the "masters of numbers", it can be a valid strategy to start looking at the architecture like an open artwork, overwritable and flexible. It is necessary to follow the footsteps of our big historical heritage, studying the principles and the archetypes, which are authentic references for the research, but also traces for their valorisation.

The reference for the construction and the interpretation of the theo-

ries for the cities relies on the "footsteps of the giants", which have
been used the common sense without determinism, following the
path of "spontaneous sustainability", carelessly of definitions, numbers and slogans.

Starting from the abovementioned
concepts, it has been produced a
series of three iconic images, three
potential solutions to nightmare,
utopia and a different city's imagi-
nation.

The first image represents an
underground architecture constructed by hypogaeus rooms dug
in the ground, while the second represents a tree-architecture made
up of rooms on branches, reproducing a house for the sustainability's
dream. At the end, the third solution sees the reconnection as solution, almost like in the anastylosis
of broken columns, which by means of the recomposition process
can be reconnected, as far as it has
been proposed to reflect on the
existing to connect it to the future
transformations.

IMAGES

1. Pettorruso, A., Lucubration and Hypo-
chondria, like anamorphic scenarios of the
city.
2. Pettorruso, A., Underground world, solution to the "nigthmare of global warming",
taking to the extreme the right side cover
image.
3. Pettorruso, A., Tree-house, solu
tion to the "sustainable utopia" and "green
invasion", taking to the extreme the left side
cover image.
4. Pettorruso, A., Reconnections, icon of
third solution, that it is not represented in
cover image.

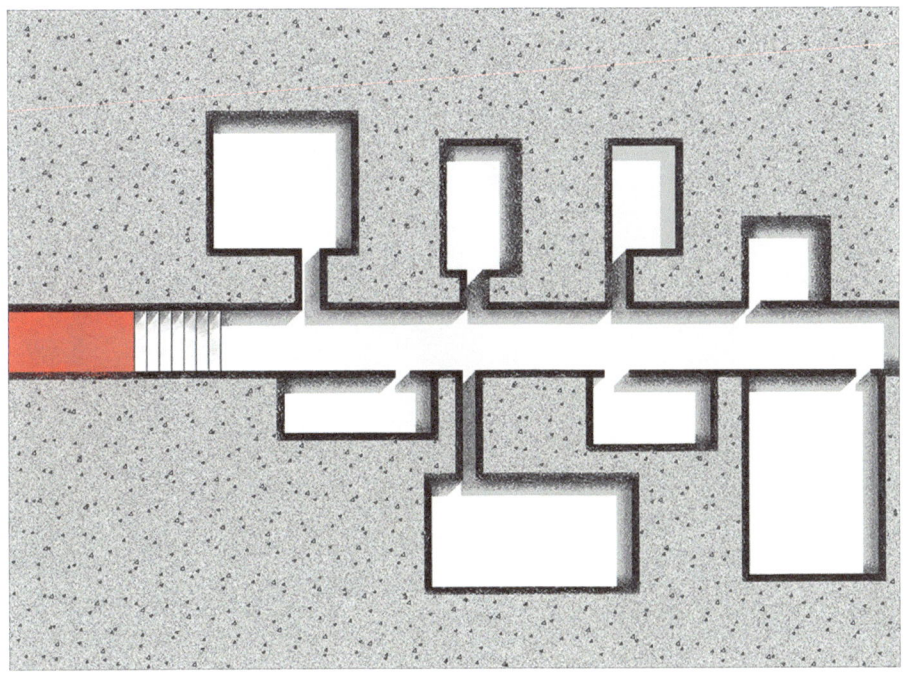

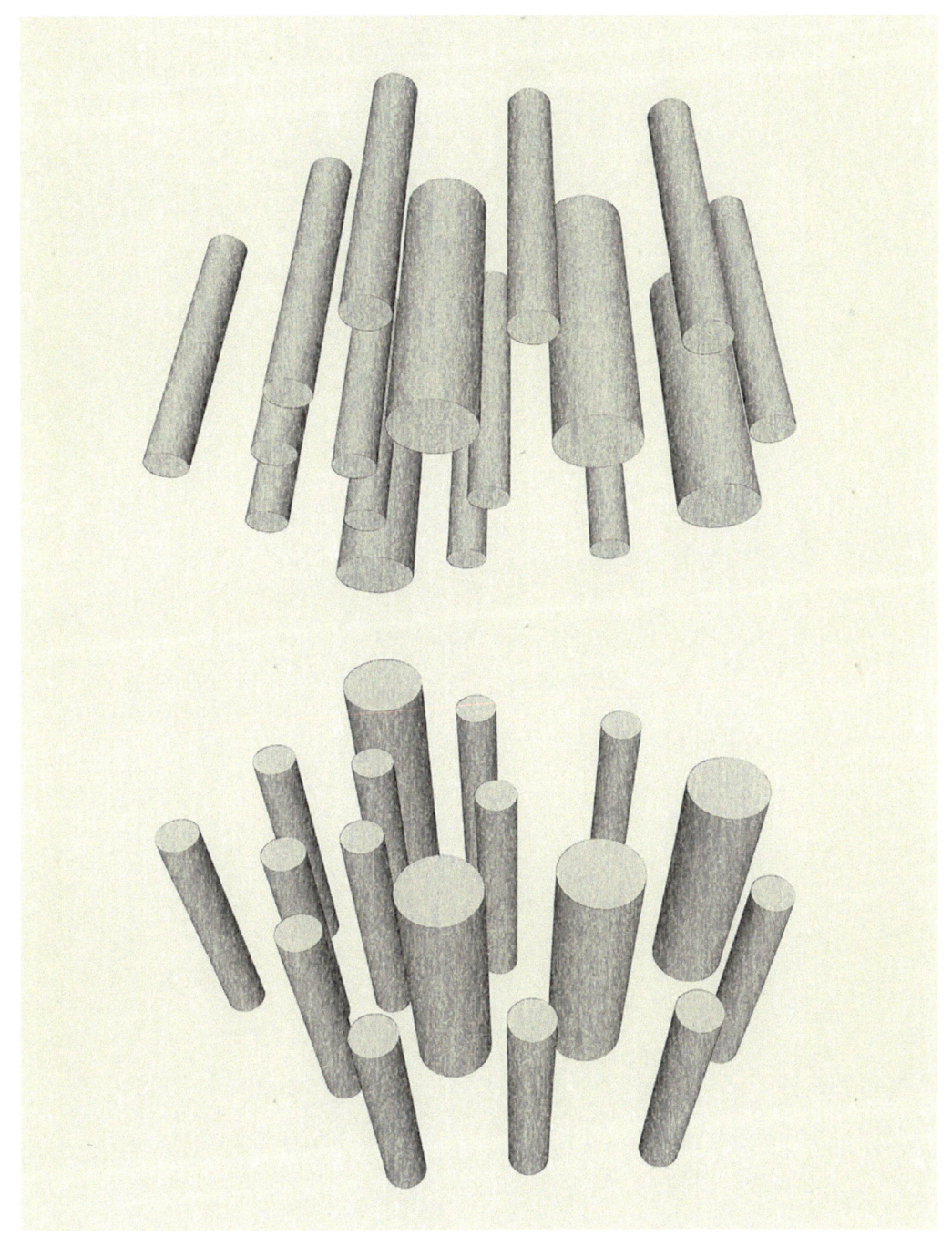

VISIONS

Bild
Nord/Sud

Chiara Giorgetti, Professor

The use of out-of-date systems considered obsolete in contemporary art is a conscious choice to rethink a medium while transforming the represented images. The starting point is a photographic shot made on film and finally digitized through numerous printing steps in the darkroom. The final print realized with the plotter sets a visual structure that is distant from the original image, afterwards it is re-elaborated with the drawing and with autograph text. The cognitive process of handwriting thus makes it possible to enter an imaginary boundary line in the function of the work itself, reinterpreting its meaning. In this way there is a sort of disorientation that transforms real places into inner worlds, a line of demarcation and a shift of coordinates.

Author Bio

Chiara Giorgetti (1963) is professor at the Academy of Fine Arts of Brera, Milan. Her artwork ranges across a wide variety of media, revolving around the subjects of communication, time and memory, and human powerlessness in a technology-dominated environment. Since the 80's she has participated in international exhibitions, lectures, workshops, and has collaborated with numerous magazines and websites. From 2001 to 2011 she managed Printshow.it a webzine that connected the Italian printmaking scene with the practice of contemporary art. Since 2012 she is co-curator of da>verso, a project on the poetry and art languages.

http://chiaragiorgetti.wordpress.com

Untitled

HACKATAO

I hate Cities because they do not have enough rounded corners, with all those straight lines that amplify my astigmatism. I hate Cities because they are a concentrate of "too much", a bulimic drainage of energy and waste. Unnatural human devices that demean the human being. They are a legacy of an insecure and closed civilization, which masturbates with fantasies in the dry chthonic of concrete, ejaculating appearances of concreteness. But there is nothing more ephemeral than a city, since all life develops over the death of other places. Cities stink of ruin, snore, snort puke up beings diluted. Cities are in the same topic. Then they are not anymore. Cities have no Humus and will starve.

Authors Bio

Nifty "borderliner" Hackatao blends cultured quotes from the past to courageous and ultra-contemporary forms, standing as an innovative exponent of the current art scene. The Hackatao art duo consists of Sergio Scalet (1973 Transacqua – TN) and Nadia Squarci (1977-Udine).
The duo was formed in Milan in 2007 by working together on the creation of Podmork, sculptures with soft and totemic shapes, which are placed at the focal centre of their imaginative research

Untitled

邱惠眉 *Huimei Chiu*

Author Bio

STUDIO SING IN THE RAIN

Working as a graphic designer, specialized in book design, identity design, and editorial design, meanwhile being a Japanese to Chinese interpreter in the fields of art and design.
Engaged in independent publications in Taiwan, Japan and Korea.

https://www.behance.net/user/?username=studiosingintherain

Alias Idem

Fabrizio Ferraro

Alias idem is a sequence of photographic works focused on the relationship between reality and its reflection. Elements from urban contemporary architecture are reflected and rotated, literally giving life to parallel dimensions, places at first invisible but somehow already existing in the reality that originates them, yet visible but inexistent once manifested. Space contains endless alternative versions of itself: final image is determined by the positioning of the mirror plane that, as a two-dimensional mirror cutting through reality, creates the illusion of a three-dimensional equivalent space that exists somewhere, yet not there. It happens that the same place can open outwards with a wide breath or close in on itself, living of an interstitial and underground, more intimate nature. Reflection, therefore, not only as mirroring but also as rethinking, re-elaborating visible to unveil the invisible.

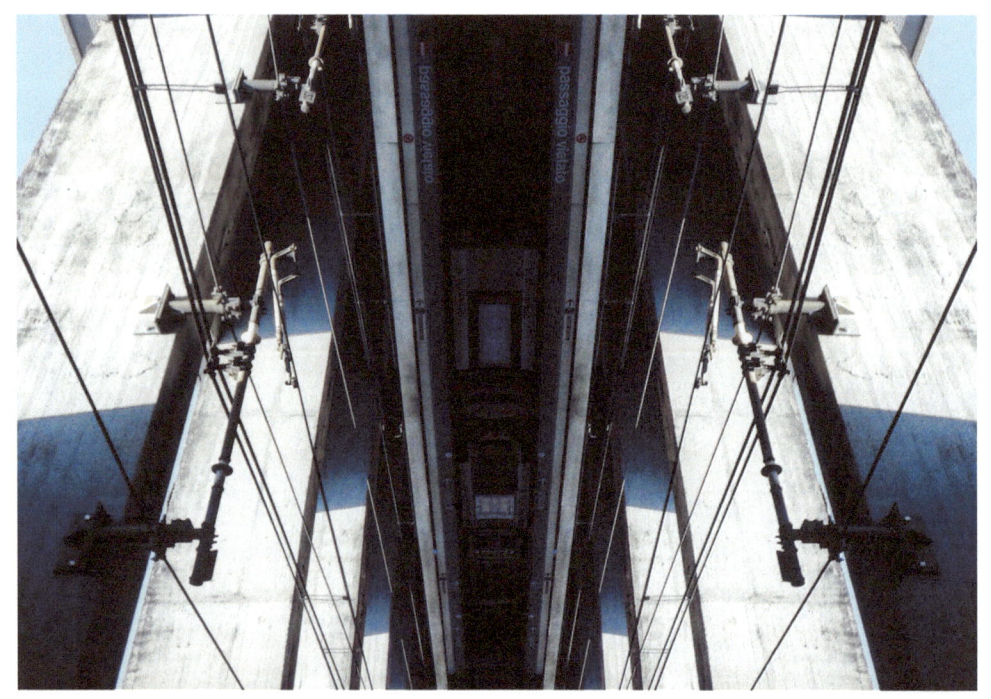

Houses

Fabio Fabiani

Author Bio

Fabio Fabiani was born in Spoleto, 1981. He graduates with honors at the Faculty of Architecture Valle Giulia, Sapienza Università di Roma (Rome 2007) with the professor Franco Purini. His work consist to design new buildings and architectural renovation, national and international contests of ideas, interior design and drawings of architecture. Since 2008 he collaborates with the architecture firm Abaco, Spoleto.
He realize digital drawings for art exhibitions and for the presentation of projects with fotorealistic pictures.
His personal exhibitions are "Designing the height of the Sky" 2013, "The Silence of Mental Places" 2015; he has been one of the selected artists for the art exhibition "Spoleto Contemporanea" Palazzo Collicola Arti Visive Spoleto 2016 and "Roma allo Specchio" Palazzo Lucarini Contemporary Trevi 2017.
He is co-founder of OFARCH Officina d'Architettura and since 2015 he is the coordinator of La Casa dell'Architettura Spoleto
www.fabiofabiani.com
www.ofarchspoleto.it

The sections to live.

The "Houses" project represents architectural visions where human habitation is measured by the contour-limit spaces of the section.

These sectioned spaces allow to show outside the inside microcosm, that is to say the daily and absolute space connection.

"Through the part we see the whole" is the rule applied. Hardly touched on rooms, openings, passages are a symbol of the human mind's uncertenty in its transition from idea to drawing to final realization.
O1 and O2 houses are organized in and through the contact between the vertical-pillars of gravity lines and spacial boxes. In the O3 House whereas the line writhes free in depth and along a path of pure volumetric forms.
The three drawings are to be read as three stations within which it is possible to observe that beside composition's harmony there is also the clearing of silence wrapping up the materic sign.

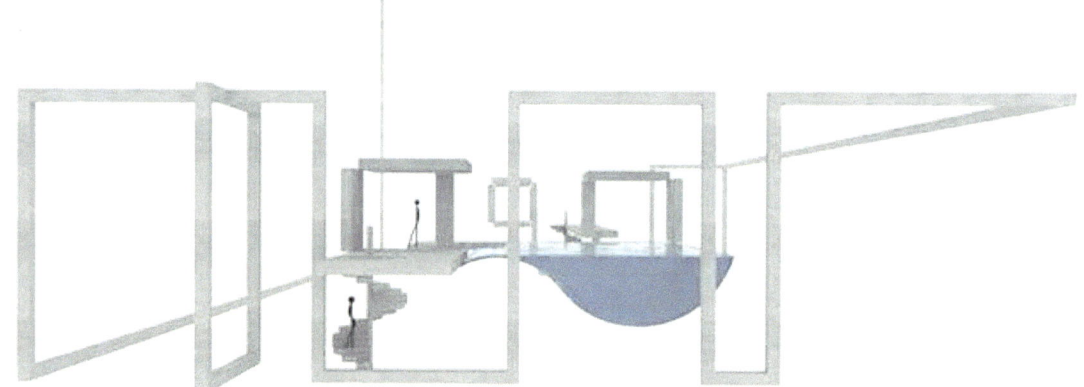

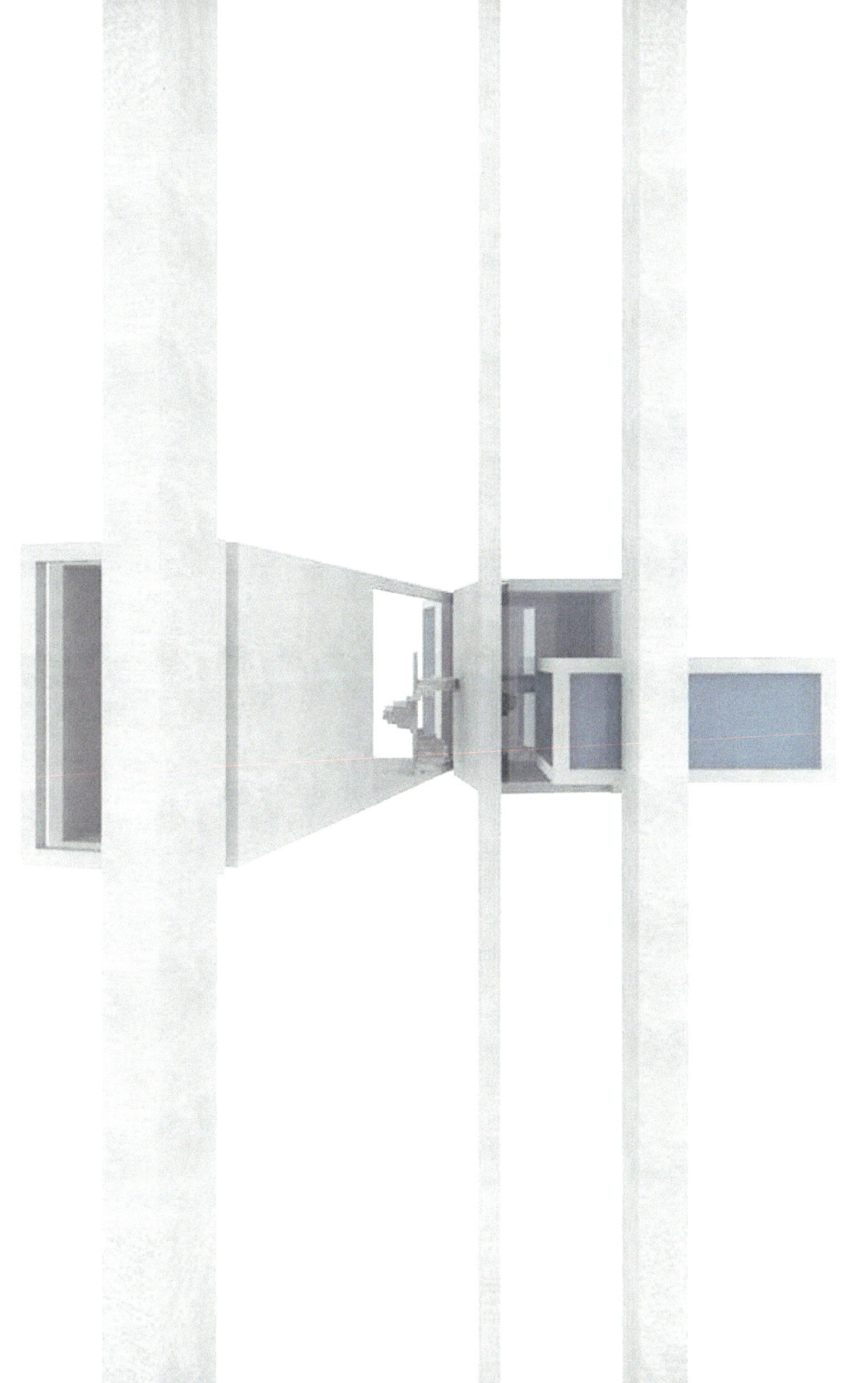

Camera di un sezionatore

Nicola Vazzoler

Author Bio

Architect, PhD in Urban Policies and Local Project (dissertation: "Urban intensity, a reasoned report starting from the case of Rome" - 2015) now is Research fellow at Rome Tre University. He did educational work and research at the Universities of Trieste, IUAV and RomaTre (including the Inter-university research "Fifty years of planning standards" and the Research project of national interest "Post-metropolitan territories as emerging urban forms"). As a professional, he did research and participated in the drafting process of a number of urban development plans (including: "Plan of the Archaeological Monumental Area of the Colosseum" for RomaTre University). He is co-founder of GU | Generazione Urbana (last work: "Monitoring of contemporary peripheral forms in Rome" for the Italian Ministry of Cultural Heritage and Activities) and he is deputy editor of UrbanisticaTre an online scientific journal of urban studies (peer review journal).

Layering represents an elemental form of decomposition (with subsequent recomposition) that is placed between pre-defined categories and new representations (Viganò, P. 1999. La città elementare, Skira, Milan).

These are the assumptions of "Camera di un sezionatore" that wants to put on the same level a possible reading made with layers of the Metropolitan City of Rome (here represented at the bottom through a deconstruction articulated around simple elements, from the left: road system; the buildings; the railway system; the water system; the green areas) and other representations that tell one or more stories about the city of Rome, or parts of it, different sections of the city.

These sections (different in languages and techniques of construction) show, in sequence, the transformations of the city: from small urban agglomeration (in Nolli map of 1748 was smaller than the Aurelian Walls) Rome becomes a metropolis through turbulent processes in its peripheral areas ("Uccellacci e uccellini" by Pier Paolo Pasolini in 1966 or "Brutti, sporchi e cattivi" by Ettore Scola in 1976 show the transformation of the Roman suburbs, the "borgate" and his inhabitants), passing through the transformation of his hystorical center started in 1871 (Rome became Capital) and followed under the Fascist regime (among them: the banks of the Tiber, called "muraglioni"; the elimination of "Campo Vaccino"; the elimination of the Alessandrino and Velia neighborhood and "Spina di borgo"; realization of Eur; etc.) and the Second World War.

The path described imposes a change of scale: from the "center" of Rome to its wide territory (from Ostia to Fiano Romano, from Valmontone to Fregene) where part of the urban materials of the city of Rome and its ways of life sedimented (or are still sedimenting) and where live most of its population and city users. It's a necessary to think about the future of the city ("Roma 20-25" by MAXXI Architettura and Comune di Roma which moves from the collective project "Roma Interrotta" of 1978), because the rest of territory is Rome: "even if boundless, infinite, undone and so on, we continue to call cities with the old names: New York, Las Vegas, Los Angeles, Shanghai, Mexico City, Mumbai, Hanoi, Moscow, London, Rome" (Pasqui G. 2017. Urbanistica oggi. Donzelli. Roma).

Toys(e/a)ction#1

Anna Riciputo

Author Bio

https://utopiaspa.wordpress.com

Untitled

Denis Pitter

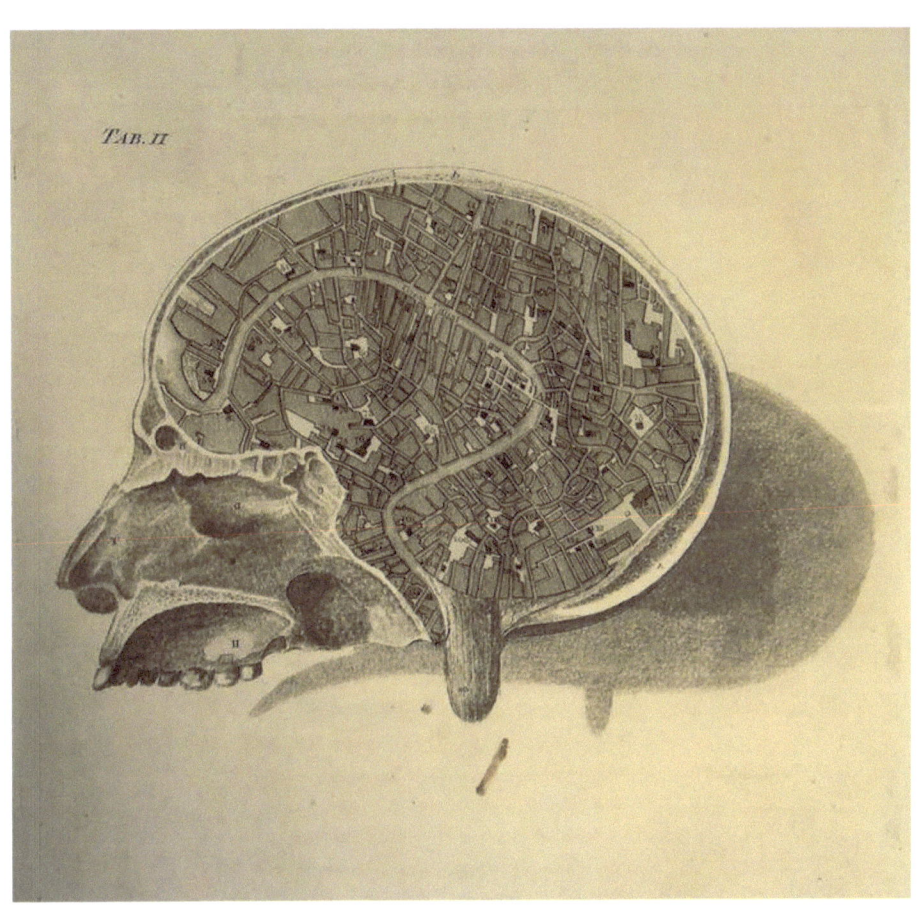

Morphosis 001

Clelia Dri

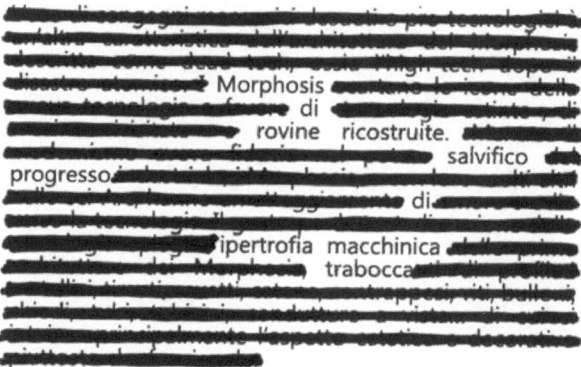

POETICA DELLE TECNOLOGIE ESTINTE.

Morphosis
di
rovine ricostruite.
salvifico
progresso
di
ipertrofia macchinica
trabocca

LE METAFORE DEL SUOLO.

esplora
il suolo   dove
tutto è
manipolato
oscilla fra   forme che
mascherano,   conformat
l'astrazione
della forma e dello spazio,
suolo (ground
da cui   emerge
un'architettura   vissuta

Any colour you like in middle land

Dario Ragona
2016

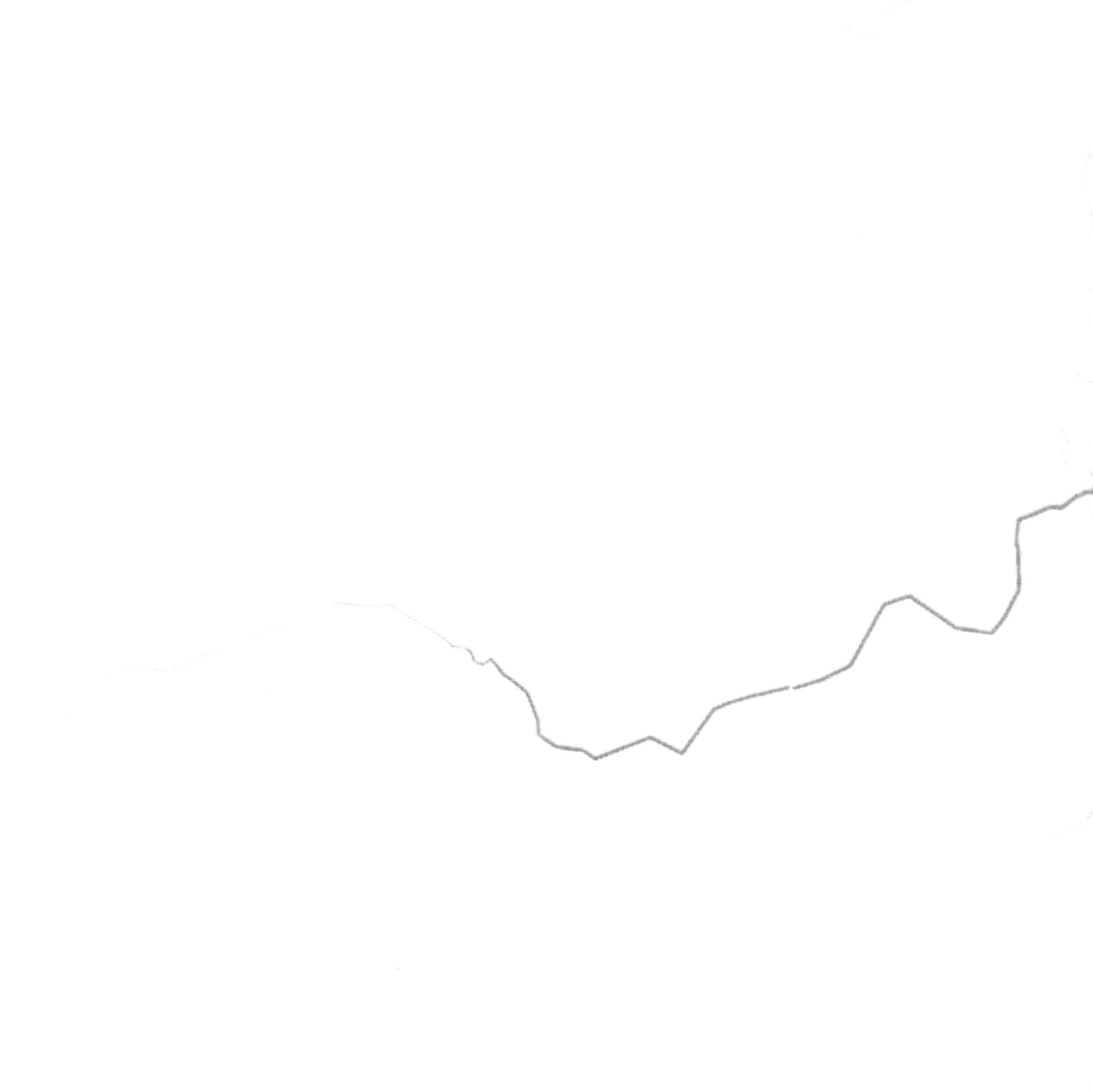

URBAN
CORPORIS

THE CITY WITHIN

Lightning Source UK Ltd.
Milton Keynes UK
UKHW050345030822
406761UK00002B/38